# SEX MATTERS
# FOR COLLEGE
# STUDENTS

# SEX MATTERS

## FOR COLLEGE STUDENTS

### FAQs in Human Sexuality

**SANDRA L. CARON, PH.D**

*The University of Maine*

PEARSON

Prentice Hall

Upper Saddle River, New Jersey 07458

Library of Congress Cataloging-in-Publication Data

Caron, Sandra L.
    Sex matters for college students: FAQs in human sexuality / Sandra L.
Caron—2nd ed.
        p. cm.
    Includes bibliographical references.
    ISBN 0-13-173426-1
    1. Sex instruction. 2. Sexual ethics. 3. College students—Sexual behavior. I.
Title.

    HQ35.2.C37 2005
    613.9′6—dc22

                                                            2005044770

**Editorial Director:** Leah Jewell
**Executive Editor:** Jessica Mosher
**Editorial Assistant:** William Grieco
**Director of Marketing:** Brandy Dawson
**Senior Marketing Manager:** Jeanette Moyer
**Marketing Assistant:** Alexandra Trum
**Assistant Managing Editor (Production):** Maureen Richardson
**Production Liaison:** Maureen Richardson
**Manufacturing Buyer:** Sherry Lewis
**Cover Design:** Karen Salzbach
**Composition/Full-Service Project Management:** GGS Book Services/Donna Lurker
**Printer/Binder:** R.R. Donnelley & Sons

Pearson Education, Ltd.
Pearson Education Australia PTY, Limited
Pearson Education Singapore, Pte., Ltd.
Pearson Education North Asia Ltd.
Pearson Education, Canada, Ltd.
Pearson Educación de Mexico, S.A. de C.V.
Pearson Education–Japan
Pearson Education Malaysia, Pte., Ltd.
Pearson Education, Upper Saddle River, NJ

PEARSON
Prentice
Hall

10 9 8 7 6 5 4 3 2 1
ISBN 0-13-173426-1

# CONTENTS

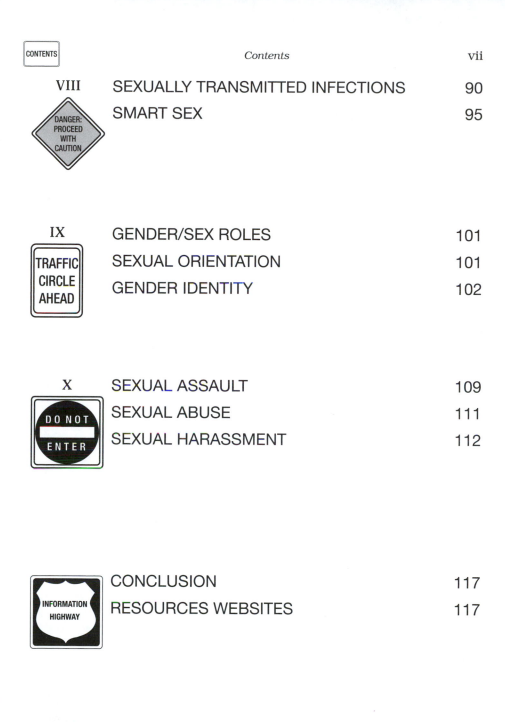

ENTER

As complete human beings we are composed of many parts, each of which is complemented by others. Sexual feelings and responses are important parts of ourselves; being aware of and understanding them can be a very valuable part of our self-discovery.

This book was designed to help you become aware of and understand your sexual feelings and responses, to accept these feelings in yourself, and to enhance your life. It is designed to assist you on your own sexual journey. It includes information on a variety of sexual topics, as well as sample questions from other college students just like you.

As you will see from reading the questions in this book, sexuality goes far beyond sexual intercourse. It is the complete range of our ideas and feelings in dealing with others and being comfortable with ourselves. Satisfaction concerning our sexuality is a lifelong process that is built upon self-esteem and mutual respect.

Thus, sexual expression is an experience that is fulfilling when it is performed by partners who are mutually willing to accept responsibility for their actions. This includes an open discussion of not only when it is agreeable to become sexually active, but also of pregnancy and disease prevention prior to sexual intercourse. It's important to remember that sexual intercourse always involves the risk of pregnancy and disease since nothing is 100% effective. Mature partners take this into consideration.

Sex, in these terms, is not something that should be connected with guilt. There is nothing wrong with expressing one's feelings sexually in an equal, open relationship. Sex with just anyone, on the other hand, can be emotionally unsatisfying, because it is, at most, a temporary means of satisfaction.

We should never allow ourselves to be used as sex objects or to be pressured by girlfriends, boyfriends, or peers. We owe it to ourselves to share this intimacy only with people whom we truly care about and who care about us. If we share a caring relationship, we'll understand if one of us is not ready or chooses to abstain.

Overall, sex can be a wonderful shared experience between mutually caring partners. The best way to a good sex life is to accept our own sexuality, to realize that all of our fantasies and thoughts are normal, and to share ourselves with our partners.

This book serves as a road map to help you enjoy your sexual journey. It contains the most frequently asked questions I have received over my many years of college teaching. As a professor of human sexuality, I have had the opportunity to study and work with these issues directly. A strength of this book is that it contains questions obtained directly from students—both males and females—and covers the range of classes from first-year students to seniors in college. The questions have been organized into sections by topic areas. The book uses traffic signs to delineate the various sections:

 stresses the importance of stopping to gain some basic understanding before proceeding;

 emphasizes cautionary limits;

 deals with sexual thoughts and behaviors;

discusses decisions that are permanent and can't be reversed;

 focuses on joining, shared lives, and dating;

 is about resolving problematic situations;

 focuses on those things that are real dangers and those things that you should be aware of in order to have a pleasant sexual experience;

 deals with the various sexually transmitted infections and the importance of smart sex;

 has to do with choice and various directions and with where you want to be;

 deals with sexual assault, abuse, and harassment;

provides you with ideas for finding out more, recognizing that your sexuality can be a lifelong journey.

Sandra L. Caron, Ph.D.

**I**

## SEXUAL ORGANS

Although women's external sexual anatomy may vary greatly in appearance, the internal organs within each woman's body are the same in the sense that they all perform the same functions. Each month an egg is released from one of the ovaries and passes into one of the fallopian tubes. This occurs approximately two weeks before menstruation. During this time the uterus has been preparing for a possible pregnancy by thickening and engorging its lining with mucus and blood vessels. If an egg is fertilized by a sperm, it will move from the tube to the uterus where it will attach itself on the uterine wall and thus pregnancy begins. If the egg is not fertilized, it will decompose *en route* to the uterus and approximately two weeks later the lining will be shed through the cervix and out through the vagina as menstrual flow. This cycle takes approximately 28 days but varies from woman to woman and within each individual.

Just as women's sexual organs may vary in appearance, men's external organs also may vary. The scrotum, located at the base of the penis, contains both testicles. Sperm is continually produced in the testes and then moves into the epididymis for storage. When the male becomes sexually aroused, the sperm passes through to the vas deferens, and the penis becomes erect. A drop of seminal fluid is released at this time. Upon ejaculation sperm and seminal fluid are released with the aid of muscular contractions. Between 200 and 500 million sperm are released upon the first ejaculation, and the number decreases with each successive ejaculation. The sperm count returns to normal within 72 hours.

## SEXUAL HEALTH

It is important that you take care of your body. Your genitals are part of your body and they need care just as much as the rest of your body does. There are things that you can and should do yourself to monitor your health. For a woman this includes a monthly breast self-examination and an annual gynecological examination. For a man a monthly testicular self-examination and a regular prostate examination are recommended.

### THE BREAST EXAM

Women should examine their breasts once a month, usually following menstruation, in search of abnormal lumps. A woman who is familiar with her own breasts can detect abnormalities much more efficiently than a medical provider can because she is more aware of her own body and the way it should feel. While most breast lumps are found to be benign, there is a much higher rate of recovery in women with malignant lumps who regularly examine their breasts than in those women who do not examine themselves. Breast cancer is the second most common form of cancer in women. It should also be noted that 1 in 100 cases of breast cancer occur in men; therefore, men should also examine their breasts on a regular basis.

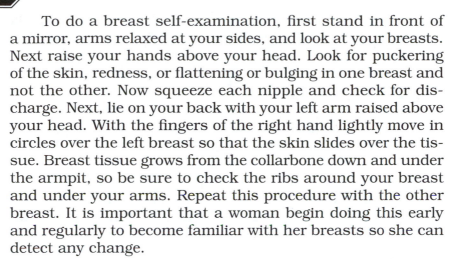
To do a breast self-examination, first stand in front of a mirror, arms relaxed at your sides, and look at your breasts. Next raise your hands above your head. Look for puckering of the skin, redness, or flattening or bulging in one breast and not the other. Now squeeze each nipple and check for discharge. Next, lie on your back with your left arm raised above your head. With the fingers of the right hand lightly move in circles over the left breast so that the skin slides over the tissue. Breast tissue grows from the collarbone down and under the armpit, so be sure to check the ribs around your breast and under your arms. Repeat this procedure with the other breast. It is important that a woman begin doing this early and regularly to become familiar with her breasts so she can detect any change.

## THE GYNECOLOGICAL EXAM

When she reaches the age of 18 or becomes sexually active, a woman should have a gynecological checkup once a year. The purpose of the exam is to look for signs of possible infection, cancer, and abnormalities that might otherwise go undetected and cause serious complications. In the examination room the medical provider will begin by giving the woman a check of vital signs, usually blood pressure and heart rate. Then, the woman lies on her back while her breasts, upper abdomen, vulva, and anus are examined for swelling or tenderness. Next, a speculum will be inserted into the vagina to hold the vaginal walls open to check the cervix. Most women do not find the insertion of the speculum painful although it may be uncomfortable. With the cervix visible, the medical provider will check the vaginal mucus color and do a pap smear. A pap smear is done by scraping a few cells from the cervix for lab analysis. This procedure is painless and in many cases the woman does not even realize that it is taking place. A test for possible infection may also be done by collecting mucus with a cotton swab.

In the last step of the gynecological exam, the medical provider removes the speculum and inserts a sterile gloved finger into the vagina and presses down on the lower abdomen with the other hand. This procedure checks the position of the ovaries, fallopian tubes, and uterus, looking for any lumps or inflammation. The examination is now over. Be sure to ask the medical provider any questions that you may have.

## THE TESTICULAR EXAM

Cancer of the testes mainly affects men between the ages of 20 and 40. It is not common, but since there are no symptoms, it is important for men to check the testicles for lumps, tenderness, hardening, or enlargement. Every month after a warm bath or shower a man should use his fingertips and thumbs and feel each testicle individually. Any irregularities should be checked by a medical provider immediately.

## THE PROSTATE EXAM

Prostate cancer is the most common form of cancer among men. If detected early, it has a very high cure rate. Early detection requires a digital rectal-prostate exam, which is recommended for men every year after the age of 30. By inserting a gloved finger into the rectum, the medical provider can feel for irregular or unusually firm areas on the prostate that may indicate a tumor.

It is important to take care of your body. These simple steps can help ensure a healthy and fulfilling life. Take time to be concerned about your body—it's the only one you have.

## BODY IMAGE

*She's so pretty, why is she seeing him? She could do*
*so much better.*
*He's gorgeous! I don't have a chance.*
*Look at that body! I'd kill to go out with her.*

Our body image has a lot to do with how we feel about ourselves and how we relate sexually to others. The society in which we live often measures goodness by beauty and conveys the message that people who are more attractive are more desirable. "She's a beautiful girl. Everyone loves her."

This interpretation of bodies plays a large part in how we feel about sexual attractiveness. If we feel good about ourselves, we're generally more open to sexual expression. If a person has a pimple or has gained a few pounds, he or she tends to feel unattractive and embarrassed. Often at the start of a new relationship we spend a great deal of time apologizing for our bodies, making excuses for this or that. Someone who feels good about himself or herself is relaxed and seems open to other people.

Few of us have perfect bodies. Each one of us is different and each has insecurities about one's body. There is no perfect way to be. Everyone is a balance of characteristics and it is the inner dimension of the individual that creates the ultimate basis of all relationships. What people fail to recognize in their efforts to achieve "the look" is that you can't have a relationship with a breast or a penis. Relationships are based on mutual appreciation of each other's values, gifts, and warmth.

Learn to see yourself for all that you are rather than all that you are not.

## FAQS

1. **Which is better in a penis: length or width? Male, First-Year**

   *Most women say penis size is not important to them in a sexual relationship. They are more concerned about their male partner taking his time and about his total response to her during sexual intercourse. The quality of the entire relationship (not the size of the penis) appears to be the most important factor in sexual enjoyment and satisfaction. You may have heard the quote, "It's not the size of the boat, but the motion of the ocean." The vagina is quite adept at accommodating to penis size and many women actually prefer stimulation around the clitoris and vaginal opening to deep thrusting, which some women may find painful. Pleasant stimulation doesn't require a large penis (in width or length) and can be achieved by hand or mouth. The size of a man's penis seems to be more important in the locker room than in the bedroom.*

## 2. What is the average size of a penis (really!!)? Male, First-Year

*Woody Allen once said that he was the only man he knew who suffered penis envy. I think he was wrong. It's fairly common for men to worry about their penis size. Some people have suggested that since the growth of the penis is one of the marks of puberty, somehow an association is made between penis size and manhood. Unfortunately, men's magazines frequently advertise penis enlargers, which exploit male anxieties (and don't work, by the way!). In its unerect or unaroused state the penis is usually between 2 1/2 and 4 inches. In its erect state the penis is usually 5 to 7 inches. It's important to know there is no relationship between the size of a man's penis and his ability to have sexual intercourse or to excite his partner. A larger penis will not make a woman have an orgasm any more than a smaller one will.*

## 3. Is penis size related to body size? Female, First-Year

*You may have heard the "Thumb Rule" that says a man's penis size is related to the size of his thumb, or another myth in which it is believed that a tall, skinny man has a large penis while a man with a short, stalky build has a small penis. Sorry to disappoint you—but penis size is not correlated with the size of a man's thumb, or body build, or nose, or shoe size. You'll have to investigate more closely to ascertain the truth.*

## 4. If sperm is made up of 90% sugar, why does it taste so salty? Female, Sophomore

*Although semen usually tastes salty, it does contain fructose, a simple sugar. Semen varies in taste from man to man, and the flavor can change from time to time in one individual. Diet is thought to be one of the factors that influences taste.*

## 5. I have heard that each time a man ejaculates, his sperm count decreases. Can a man become sterile from an ultra-active sex life? Male, Junior

*Sperm are continually being produced by the testes. The sperm count does decrease after an ejaculation, but returns to normal a short time later (within 72 hours). Barring severe injury, you're likely to have a lifelong supply.*

6. **How do I know if I'm really ovulating? Female, Junior**

   *It's really hard to tell, but one can assume that with regular menstrual periods your system is working as it should. Generally, ovulation occurs in only one ovary each month, usually 10 to 16 days before the onset of the next menstrual period. Some women experience a twinge on one side of the lower abdomen during ovulation, called mittelschmerz (German for middle pain). Around the time of ovulation there is an increase and a change in cervical mucus secretions. The mucus becomes clear, slippery, and stretchy (like egg white). It is at this time that a woman can most easily become pregnant. If you really want to understand your body and your ovulatory cycle, I suggest learning natural family planning (there are books explaining this); this method teaches you how to chart your temperature and mucus changes in order to predict ovulation. You can also buy an ovulation-prediction kit at the drugstore; but this can be a bit expensive, as it requires you to check your urine daily for the presence of hormones.*

7. **How many days out of the month can a woman be impregnanted? Male, Junior**

   *A woman is technically only fertile for approximately 1 day; that is, the day she ovulates. The egg is generally fertilizable for only 12 to 24 hours following its release from the ovary. Ovulation typically occurs 14 days before the start of her next menstrual cycle. Because sperm only have an effective life of about 72 hours and the egg an even shorter life, conception must occur within 24 to 36 hours of ovulation. Knowing this, it is amazing to think people are even able to get pregnant.*

8. **What does it mean to have a "tipped" uterus? Female, Junior**

   *The uterus is held in the pelvic area by ligaments—sort of suspended in place. It is generally perpendicular to the vagina. However, in 1 in every 10 women, the uterus tilts back (hence, the term tipped), which poses no serious problems but may cause discomfort in some positions during intercourse.*

9.  **What is the clitoris and why is it so important? Male, Sophomore**

    *In the female, it is the small erectile, hooded organ at the front of the vulva whose sole function is sexual pleasure. The clitoris has many nerve endings and is highly sensitive to sexual stimulation. Adequate stimulation (orally, manually, or indirectly through intercourse) plays an important role in a woman's ability to reach orgasm.*

10. **Can a woman have sex while she is menstruating? Male, First-Year**

    *Yes, and many women do. Some women even prefer intercourse during this time because they fear pregnancy less (assuming they ovulate in the middle of their cycle). Having sex/orgasm often makes a women feel particularly good at this time and can relieve menstrual cramping by relieving pelvic congestion. While some women feel more sexual during this period, others wouldn't dream of desiring sex while menstruating. Although sex during her period is harmless, a woman's attitude about menstruation can affect how she (or her partner) feels about participating in sex during this time.*

11. **My boyfriend has a curved penis, which makes sexual intercourse uncomfortable. We've tried different positions, but that hasn't helped. It's really curved! What should I do? Female, Senior**

    *Unlike women, who tend to have regular gynecological exams where certain conditions are recognized and discussed, males are not so lucky. Has he ever been to see a urologist or family physician to discuss this? I would encourage him to do so, since it sounds like this is interfering with your ability to engage in intercourse. You may want to avoid sexual intercourse until he sees a specialist and focus instead on other ways to satisfy one another. While some degree of curvature is perfectly normal, men with Peyronie's disease have excessive curvature that can make erections painful or make it difficult to enjoy intercourse. Peyronie's disease is a rare condition caused by buildup of fibrous tissue and calcium deposits in the penile shaft. Although some cases appear to clear up on their own, most require medical attention. Encourage your boyfriend to talk to a doctor for a referral to a local urologist. Good luck.*

## 12. What percentage of guys have a circumcised penis? Female, Junior

*Approximately 80% of American males have a circumcised penis, whereas 80% of European males have an uncircumcised penis. The American Academy of Pediatrics used to recommend circumcision for health concerns, but in 1999 they issued a new circumcision policy noting that there is no medical evidence to suggest the need for such a procedure. Most circumcisions done today are done for religious, cultural, or aesthetic reasons. Circumcision is a required ritual in Jewish and Muslim religious practice.*

## 13. Why do some women have small breasts while others have larger ones? Female, First-Year

*Clearly, heredity plays a role, along with the amount of fatty tissue we have. No matter what their size, breasts are still capable of performing their primary function of serving as a source of milk for babies. And remember: variety is the spice of life. Just as some people have a smaller nose, others have a larger one; some have smaller feet and some have larger feet, and so on. Think how boring it would be if we all came in exactly the same size.*

## 14. My roommate told me that sex makes a woman's hips wider. Does it? Female, First-Year

*No. There is no way to tell if a woman has had sex simply by looking at her body structure/build. It is sort of amusing to think about what the world would look like if what your roommate is suggesting were true.*

## 15. Is it possible to physically stretch the penis continually in the hope that it will elongate over time? Male, Sophomore

*Possible? Yes, anything is possible. Probable? No. I am not aware of anyone using this technique successfully. So much of our anatomy is the result of genetics. Just as a person may grow up to have long or short legs, he may grow up to have a long or short penis. Heredity plays a key role in this.*

**16. Why are women made to feel unattractive if they are average-looking as opposed to model-looking? Female, First-Year**

*If by "average-looking" you mean the majority of women, then logically the majority must be attractive since they attract others and the human race continues. If only people who look like models were attractive, the birthrate would drop precipitously. Not all men look for the same characteristics, despite the messages from the media about the ideal female form. In fact, over time the ideal changes. I have a friend whose rosy gentle curves would make her an ideal in the 17th century. Relax and look for a guy whose ideal is not the media stereotype.*

**17. I'm going with my friends to Fort Lauderdale for Spring Break, but I'm really not comfortable with the way I look. My friends say I look fine—but I know I'll never find a cute guy. Help!! Female, Senior**

*If your friends are truly your friends, they wouldn't suggest that you go to Fort Lauderdale to have a "bum" time. They obviously expect you're going to have a good time. I suggest you let go of focusing on your imperfections and go and enjoy yourself with your friends. Perhaps a guy will find **you** while you are having a good time.*

**18. My friend says she feels shy about the way her vagina looks. What should she do? Female, First-Year**

*Join the club. There are many women who are a bit uncomfortable about the way their vulva/vagina looks. Unfortunately, many little girls gather negative messages about their bodies. Starting in early childhood they are taught that touching their genitals is "not nice" or "dirty," a message that is reinforced during toilet training when the little girl is told to "wipe carefully" and "clean yourself up." Little girls absorb the social message that their female genitals are ugly and unclean. Menstruation reinforces this message with "sanitary napkins" and embarrassed secrecy. Later, young women are urged to buy unnecessary vaginal sprays and douches to hide odors. Such sprays can be potentially irritating, and frequent douching can be harmful because it upsets the vagina's natural chemical balance, thus increasing susceptibility to infections.*

*Finally, given the taboo about touching and looking, many women have not taken a look at their own genitals and cannot accurately describe their own anatomy. A place for this woman to start is with a mirror and a basic drawing of the female anatomy (see any anatomy or human sexuality text). By becoming familiar with herself, hopefully she can learn to see the beauty in this part of her body.*

# II

## NO U TURN

---
**SEXUAL DECISION MAKING**
---

The decision whether or not to become sexually involved is an important and complex choice and one that is not easy to make. There are many variables to consider, but be forewarned—it's difficult to make a responsible decision in the "heat of the moment." Therefore, the decision whether or not to become sexually active should be made before the situation arises. Besides, this is a very individual decision, a choice you must make for yourself.

To make a good decision (for you) involving sexual activity, you should examine your values, goals, and the pros and cons of becoming involved. Ask yourself the following questions:

1. Under what conditions would I become sexually involved with this person? Is it, for example, important to you that you have been dating for a long time or that:

   - you feel comfortable
   - you are in a mature love situation

12

- you are not being used
- it will not hurt your relationship

Like it or not, sexual activity always *changes* a relationship. It is up to you to make sure that the change is positive and constructive.

2. If I decide to become sexually active, what things must I consider? For example:

   - the other person's feelings
   - birth control (Which method? Who's responsible?)
   - STIs: Are you both free of infection? Are you having sex only with each other?

3. If I decide not to become sexually active, what alternatives are available? In other words, can I have a good dating relationship without intercourse? What about:

   - kissing
   - fondling
   - oral sex
   - mutual masturbation
   - massage

It is important to note that not everybody is "doing it" and that the decision to have sex is totally yours. Just remember, this decision whether or not to become sexually active involves forethought-before-foreplay and consideration of both your own and your partner's feelings. Don't let others make your decision for you. It's yours and yours alone to make.

## VIRGINITY

If intimacy equals sex, as some believe, then people who don't engage in sexual intercourse are automatically defined as leading very dull lives. With this argument, virginity is then a state we want to leave. This view is too simplistic, only serving to pressure people to have sexual intercourse.

It is important to remember that virginity, like sexual activity, is a matter of choice. Some men and women choose to wait until they are in what they consider a long-term relationship before they become sexually involved and some do not.

Being a virgin does not mean you are not sexual or that you do not have an intimate relationship; virginity is an acceptable alternative to sexual intercourse. What is best for you is for you alone to decide.

## FIRST EXPERIENCE WITH SEXUAL INTERCOURSE

Whether it's your first time having sex or the first time with a new partner, the experience of sexual intercourse may not be as enjoyable as anticipated. How well things go depends not so much on the sexual techniques but on how we feel about the timing of the sexual intimacy and about loosening up with someone new. In general, people tend to feel somewhat anxious and strange at a first encounter. Many worry that the new partner will not find their body attractive and their "performance" sexually appealing. Some men worry that they may not have an erection or will ejaculate too quickly; some women feel so tense with a new partner that they don't have orgasm. Both may worry that they'll perform poorly in comparison with other lovers.

One way to reduce this anxiety is to postpone sex until you are comfortable with the other person and until your conditions for good sex are met. Even if the other person is interested in sex, you have the right to say no and to have your refusal accepted. Even if it is not wildly passionate or technically skillful, first sexual intercourse between people who are gentle, caring, and trusting with each other may be deeply gratifying. Most people remember their first time. Be sure it is an experience you want to remember.

## FAQS

1. **I am a virgin and my boyfriend isn't. He says it's okay that we're not having sex, but my friends say our relationship will never last. Should I be concerned? Female, Sophomore**
   *Since every person is unique, every relationship is unique. If you and your boyfriend are comfortable with your*

relationship, why worry about what your friends say? If you're not comfortable, I suggest you may want to talk it over with your boyfriend rather than your friends. It's ultimately up to you and him what you decide.

2. **If I were to believe in no sex before marriage, how would I know the man I was to marry would be sexually compatible for me? Female, Senior**

*Sexual compatibility has little to do with the performance per se. Instead, I would want to know how compatible you are in your relationship. For example, is he sensitive to your needs? Does he respect your feelings? Is he able to listen to what you have to say without becoming defensive? Does he like to do things for you? Can you communicate with him? Are you in touch with what you want and do you feel comfortable expressing your needs and desires? Again, I am referring to things that happen in your relationship generally—not just sexually. I believe compatibility has more to do with how well you relate to one another in general in various circumstances. If you truly are right for each other, the sexual mechanics will be resolved with time and experience.*

3. **My girlfriend is younger than me—she's only in her first year of college. How do I impress upon her that it is the right time to have sex? How do I tell her that now is the right time? Male, Senior**

*I suggest you approach this carefully. It may be true that **you** feel it is the right time to become sexually involved. However, this may not be where she is right now—she may not feel ready. Why not talk to her about how you are feeling, allowing her room to decide for herself if she is ready also?*

4. **Is it true that after 12 months without sex you will become a virgin again? Male, Sophomore**

*You may feel like one—but no. According to Webster's Dictionary, a virgin is someone who has never engaged in sexual intercourse. It doesn't mention anything about a time line.*

5. **Why are guys embarrassed to admit to being virgins? Female, Sophomore**

   *We give many, many social messages to boys as they are growing up to be competent, to be knowledgeable, and to be in charge—in such areas as sports, social performance, and so on. Thus, in this way, young men assume they are supposed to know and be competent in everything—even in sexual matters—before they have the experience. Everyone is a beginner sometime. There is a first time and that can be very special.*

6. **How do you know if you're ready for sex? I'm in a relationship and would like to be more involved sexually— but I'm not sure. Should I just wait until something happens or what? Male, Sophomore**

   *The right time varies from person to person, depending on your values and beliefs. Some people feel the only appropriate time to become sexually involved is after the couple is in a committed relationship (e.g., married), while others feel no commitment is necessary; in fact, knowing their sexual partner's name may not even be important.*

   *If you are unsure about when to become sexually involved, you may want to spend time talking this over with your partner. If you are unsure, it is always better to err on the side of waiting, rather than rushing into something you may regret later. Certainly, any sexual relationship should be based on mutual consent. Some other guidelines indicating you might be ready for sex include:*

   - *You're ready for sex if you're not trying to prove your love, increase your self-worth, prove you're mature, or rebel against parents or society.*
   - *You're ready for sex if it will be an expression of your current feelings rather than an attempt to improve a poor relationship or one that is growing old.*
   - *You're ready for sex if you can discuss and agree on an effective method of birth control and share the details, responsibilities, and costs.*
   - *Finally, you are ready for sex if you can discuss sexually transmitted infections, including HIV, and provide protection.*

*Deciding whether or not to become sexually involved is an important decision, a choice we make for ourselves. It should be a responsible one and it's yours alone. No one should force or push you into it. Don't wait until the last minute to decide; there are lots of things to consider. You decide!*

### 7. Is it wise to become sexually involved with someone before developing a relationship or falling in love with the person? Male, Junior

*I would tend to err on the side of waiting until you have established a relationship before becoming sexually involved. Otherwise, some might say that you are attempting to start a relationship "ass-backwards." Too often it causes problems. Often one person begins to question what the "genital encounter" really means: How does my partner feel? Am I really being used? Does this person like me? Where is the relationship going? Why does my sex partner want to be physically intimate when we are not yet emotionally intimate? When our ability to be intimate with another human being is limited to genital sex, it becomes boring, obsessive, and destructive.*

*Unfortunately, some people use sex to avoid intimacy. It's important to recognize that the interrelationships among love, intimacy, and friendship are not always clear. For instance, regardless of expectations beforehand, somehow sex invariably changes things in a relationship. People's moods change, and reactions after-the-act range from feeling the encounter was bad to feeling it was very good. Some people have sex shortly after meeting, and then consider getting to know each other. But the possibility of a relationship is already sabotaged by the morning after. Or, some people use sex as a test or proof of love or friendship, by saying in effect, "If you really like me, you'll have sex with me." There is widespread failure to understand that individuals get hurt because they don't feel loved. Most people would agree that it is important to become emotionally intimate before becoming sexually intimate. Things seem to work out better when people act in ways that are consistent with their feelings.*

8. **How do you decide to have sex with someone when you're torn between fear of disease and a need for closeness? Female, First-Year**

   *I would like to point out that a couple can be close or intimate without putting each other at risk for a disease. Affection and playfulness do not necessarily imply sexual involvement. In terms of sexual involvement, certainly it's hard to have a good time or enjoy yourself if you're afraid of catching a disease. Recognize that there is a continuum of behaviors you can engage in—ranging from safe to unsafe sex practices. It's helpful to take time to determine your exact position regarding the level of involvement you are comfortable with and to examine issues concerning protection. What are your limits? For example, "I will only have sex in a committed relationship," or "I will have intercourse only with condoms," or "I will only have sex after I've gotten to know my partner over a period of time." It's a lot easier to choose what to say to your partner if you've already determined what your limits are. Following through on your decisions means being able to talk about them: It's important to talk to your partner about what feels right for you. Other practical suggestions include: talking with your partner about your sex histories, examining your partner's genitals for signs of infection, washing before and after sex, using a condom, and making an appointment for both of you to have an STI checkup. You will enjoy your sexual relationship more once you both have a clean bill of health.*

9. **After the first week of school, I'm beginning to wonder if I'm the only virgin on campus. I haven't seen my roommate since the first night! Is there something wrong with me? Female, First-Year**

   *No, there's nothing wrong with you (I'm actually feeling more concerned about your roommate!). Some men and some women choose to wait until they are in what they consider a long-term relationship before they become sexually involved and some do not. Being a virgin does not mean you are not a sexual person, or that you don't have sexual attractions, or that you can't have an intimate relationship with another person. Your choice of virginity is a very acceptable alternative. What is best for you is for you alone to decide.*

10. **I'm not sure what to do. My boyfriend and I have a great time together but in many ways we're not the same. In fact, the longer we go out, the more pronounced our differences become. He feels that it's okay to have sex before marriage, while I believe in waiting. I don't want to break up with him—but it doesn't seem possible to continue dating, if you know what I mean. Female, Sophomore**

*What you seem to be dealing with is incompatible sexual values between you and your boyfriend. Have you been able to talk with him about this? What is his opinion? Are you feeling pressured? What are the things that hold your relationship together? Are you compatible in many other areas? Compatible sexual values are an important consideration in dating. However, you should know that some couples develop and maintain a relationship in spite of differences between their sexual values. For example, a person who values sexual monogamy may become involved with a person who values sexual variety with multiple partners. Couples with conflicting sexual values may consider the following options: changing their values, changing their behavior (while retaining their values), accepting their differences, and ending the relationship. In your case, you will need to decide what is best for you. I would hope that you would be able to find the strength to hold on to those things that you feel are important and not feel pressured to change your values or behavior for the sake of saving a relationship.*

11. **If your first sexual experience wasn't what you expected, how do you become comfortable in the future with a different partner? Female, Junior**

*It will take time. I believe it means taking time to develop the kind of relationship where there is mutual respect, caring, and trust. I'm sorry that your first sexual experience was not comfortable. It would be helpful to know a bit more about what happened in order to understand what needs to happen in the future to make it better. Maybe you could think about that. In terms of future relationships, keep in mind that the context of the relationship can be crucial in determining how comfortable one feels. Take your time.*

12. **Is it true that after 7 years of not having sex your hymen can grow back, making you a virgin? Female, Sophomore**

*No, you would still not qualify as a virgin again if you didn't have sex for 7 (or 70!) years—celibate maybe, but not a virgin. A virgin refers to someone who's never had sexual intercourse. The hymen (a thin tissue membrane that covers part of the vaginal opening) has been regarded throughout history as proof of virginity. Yet the absence or presence of a hymen is unreliable as an indicator of a woman's virginity or nonvirginity. Some women are born without a hymen; others have a hymen that has been stretched or torn through normal exercise or insertion of tampons/ fingers. I'm not aware of any hymen "growing back."*

13. **Last semester I spent the night with a guy and he hasn't talked to me since. School's back and I can't bear the fact that this guy won't even acknowledge me. I'm upset about it and don't know what to do. Any suggestions? Female, Junior**

*Not every romantic interlude leads to lifetime love, just as a single conversation does not establish long friendships. If this was someone you saw regularly, you may want to ask him if he is willing to talk about it. But, in any case, it may be more useful to find someone else. Don't base your self-esteem on this single casual encounter.*

14. **Is it okay to sleep with someone just for sex, you know, to have a one-night stand? Male, First-Year**

*A lot depends on your value system. I can't answer this for you. Some things you might want to consider are: What about sexually transmitted infections? Do you always use condoms? What is the other person feeling? What are the reasons the other person is sleeping with you? What do you want in terms of a relationship with this person the next morning? Do you want to be friends? Strangers? How* do you feel about sharing this intimate part of yourself with so many others? What are you getting out of one-night stands? Relief? Joy? Confusion? In the long run, think about what kind of relationship you want with another person. Recognize that while sex can be enjoyable in a single encounter, it is generally more satisfying in the context of a meaningful relationship.

**15. What's wrong with just enjoying each other's bodies—having sex for its own sake? Do people have to be in love to do that? Male, Junior**

*Obviously, many do not, as evidenced by the fact that sex is a popular form of interaction among college students. Many couples have sex for fun, as a way to forget troubles and relieve tension. And a few couples have been known to have a terrible relationship in almost every way, but put their problems aside and have fantastic sex. Many couples cannot separate sex from all other aspects of their relationship, however, at least in the long term. Each begins to affect the other. Resentments, tensions, feelings of being used by the other, and fears in the relationship affect their sexual life. Some people who start out wanting just a fun sexual relationship often become emotionally involved without intending to do so. Emotional involvement leads to anxiety about what a relationship means, where each stands in the other's eyes, and what plans are in the future. It is hard, and unacceptable for most, to carry on a long-term relationship without emotional involvement. Recreational sex as such may not be a problem for some unattached, consenting adults on a short-term basis. However, when all sexual encounters are treated as recreational, sex becomes trivial and superficial. Many people can and do have sex without love, but many also prefer sex with love.*

**16. What is promiscuity? Who qualifies as promiscuous? Male, First-Year**

*Someone once said, "A promiscuous person is someone who has sex more than you do." However, most people would agree that sexual promiscuity means having sex indiscriminately without much thought in the selection of a partner—loveless, random sex. It might be the person who has a different sexual partner every night of the week or every weekend—someone who does not seem interested or able to establish a relationship with another outside the bedroom. For many people who fall into this category, loveless random sex is often a way of coping with loneliness, isolation, emptiness, and previous rejection. Unfortunately, the more random sex people have, the lonelier they tend to feel, thus pulling themselves into a downward spiral of loneliness and emptiness. Promiscuity is not seen as a result of a person's strong sex drive, but as an attempt to cope with emotional problems. It's important to see promiscuity for what it is and to reach out and offer your support to friends who may be acting out their feelings in this way. They need your support, not ridicule.*

**17. How do I know if I'm promiscuous or just normally enjoying sex with several partners? Female, Junior**

*Promiscuity is a label that some people use to describe the behavior of those who have sex with a variety of different partners on a casual basis. Because of the double standard, it's more often used in a negative way to describe women. Clearly there are some people who enjoy sex with a variety of partners and prefer to avoid getting emotionally involved. If a person engages in this kind of behavior in a responsible, nonexploitative manner, taking appropriate steps to reduce risks of disease and pregnancy, and emerges from it without negative feelings or conflict, there is no particular reason to judge the behavior as a problem. Sometimes, however, having multiple sex partners may be motivated by something else. Many of us have probably seen people engaging in random sex for reasons that are not always positive, such as an unsatisfied personal life or lack of self-respect. Certainly some people feel a need to prove themselves. Multiple sexual encounters may also represent a means of escape or retaliation for a troubled relationship. In these cases, the person has the potential of creating more serious problems. Hopefully they can take a moment to look at their motives, talk with someone about what is going on, and develop more appropriate ways to deal with these stresses. I suggest you look at your motives for having sex and decide.*

18. **Is having several sex partners at the same time a really bad thing? Male, Sophomore**

    *That depends on how you define "bad." When you say "at the same time" do you mean literally "in bed together at the same time" or do you mean you happen to be involved sexually with more than one person (e.g., you sleep with one person one night, another person another night)? Either way, I think you're setting yourself up for something that may not be healthy—physically and psychologically. You may want to step back and evaluate your situation. You may want to begin by asking if everyone involved is an informed, consenting adult. Also, is each person protected from disease and pregnancy? From there, you may want to ask yourself about the emotional investment each person has in this relationship. What is it that you and the others are getting from this situation? The bottom line is that you must decide what is "good" or "bad" for you. And as an adult, you need to take responsibility for the decisions you make with your sexual behavior.*

19. **Is it okay not to speak to a girl after sex ever again— or is it easier for her if I simply say it was a one-shot deal, a one-night stand? Male, Senior**

    *I think honesty is probably the best policy in this case. Obviously, if you ignore her whenever you see her after your "get-together," she will take the hint and realize that the one-night stand was just that and nothing more. However, it might be a bit more manly if you could tell her. That way she would know it wasn't about her; it is about you and the way you approach sex. In fact, I think it would be even nicer if you could state your intentions **before** you end up in bed with someone—that way there isn't a question about what this means to you. For example, if she had hoped your sexual encounter would lead to something more significant, she now knows it will not; she has the information ahead of time to decide what she wants to do. You will find there might be less awkwardness the morning after.*

20. **How many people does one have to sleep with to be considered a "technical slut"? Female, Senior**

    *I'm not aware of an exact number. Many people would agree that the term can refer to either a male or female and is used to imply sexual promiscuity, meaning having sex indiscriminately without much thought in the selection of a partner. It might be a person who has a different sexual partner every night of the week or every weekend or every month. It's been used to refer to someone who doesn't seem interested or able to establish a relationship with another person outside the bedroom. It's a term that is typically used in the negative, as a putdown or as a means of social control.*

**21. How long should a guy stay with a girl after a one-night stand? I don't really have any interest in her, but I feel kind of guilty. I've continued to see her for the past 2 weeks—but it really isn't what I want to be doing. She was really just a one-night stand. Male, Senior**

*How long should you stick around for a one-night stand? One night. You've taken the first big step, which is being honest with yourself. Now you need to be honest with her. You really aren't doing her any favors by sticking around. You need to work out your guilty feelings by yourself.*

*I suggest you end the "relationship" by telling her you aren't interested in being in a serious dating relationship. Be sure to emphasize that this is about **you**, not her. I also think you need to consider talking with the next "one-nighter" ahead of time about your expectations, to avoid being in this situation again. You may also want to talk with someone such as a counselor about why you engage in a behavior that then makes you feel guilty. It sounds like it would be worth exploring.*

**22. My housemate has had sex with many girls this semester and is depressed each time after it happens because he feels "dirty." Why does he keep doing this? Male, Senior**

*I suspect your housemate is looking for something but not finding it through his method of one-night stands. Sometimes it takes people longer to figure out what is useful behavior. You can see it; he cannot. Have you tried to talk with him about your observations? It may be useful for him to know you are concerned about him. Maybe he could talk about his issues—what he's really reaching out for in these sexual encounters. As many people have learned, while sex can be enjoyable in a single encounter, it is generally more satisfying in the context of a meaningful relationship.*

23. **I'm definitely not interested in tying myself down with a permanent girlfriend right now. To be honest, with so many great-looking girls on campus, I prefer to keep my options open. My question is, with birth control so widely available, girls no longer have to fear becoming pregnant, but so many still want a guy to go through the whole dating routine before they'll sleep with you. If doing it just for the sex is good enough for guys, why isn't it the same for girls? Male, Junior**
    *I think you raise a good question. While certainly the advent of effective birth control in the 1960s (i.e., the Pill) allowed women more sexual freedom, you have to remember that no method is 100% effective. And condoms do offer terrific protection from disease, but again, there's still a tiny chance a condom could break or slip off. So, I hope you can appreciate a woman's hesitancy to risk pregnancy and disease with someone she hardly knows. Probably the most important aspect of all of this (which I believe you seem to be missing) is that terrific sex is much more likely to take place when there is a relationship between two people. I am not saying that one-night stands are never enjoyable, but they usually do not provide the best sex and they are definitely risky for everyone involved. So, if the women you meet want to form a relationship before they have sex with you, I hope you'll understand why and respect that. In many ways, they're doing it for the benefit of both of you.*

24. **I find myself attracted to my roommate's boyfriend, and he makes passes at me when she's not around. If I follow my true feelings, my friend will be hurt, *but* should I sacrifice my happiness for hers? Female, Junior**
    *In terms of your friend/roommate being hurt, I think she is being hurt already. She's seeing a guy who isn't being honest with her. And you, as her friend, are not being honest. Someone needs to start talking. In this situation, it sounds like your roommate's "boyfriend" needs to have a serious discussion with her about how he's feeling. It isn't*

*doing her any good to be led on. In addition, if you really feel strongly about developing a relationship with this guy, you'll need to talk with her about how you're feeling. It may be true that you will have to choose between your roommate and this guy. I wouldn't be surprised if you lose a roommate over this. You need to decide what's more important in the long run.*

**25. My boyfriend has been asking me to try anal intercourse with him. I'm not sure if that is something that I really want to do, but he is very persistent. Should I give in to satisfy him, or should I hold on to my morals? Female, First-Year**

*I think it's important that you do what feels right for* **you**— *not your boyfriend—whether it's anal sex or anything else. I'm more concerned about your partner's persistence—his inability to listen to you or accept your refusal—than I am about his request to try anal sex. It's your body. You decide what happens to it. As far as your concern about morals, you may find it interesting to know that many intimate relationships include a variety of sexual activities outside of the traditional "penis-in-vagina" model. Such behaviors are not considered "immoral" by most people but instead represent a wide range of sexual interests and desires.*

*In terms of anal sex, researchers have found that many men and women have attempted anal intercourse at least once. But it's certainly not for everyone. In fact in my own survey of students, most say that anal sex is acceptable for others, but they personally don't enjoy it or participate in it. Should you ever decide to try it, let me just suggest two things:* **lubrication** *and more* **lubrication**. *And of course, unless there is absolute certainty that your partner is not infected, a condom must be used for protection from disease. Also know that it is unsafe to insert a penis into the vagina or mouth following anal intercourse, since bacteria are easily transferred and may cause infection.*

# III

## MERGING TRAFFIC

## INITIATING A RELATIONSHIP

Attraction to another person is a complex phenomenon, based on prior experiences, unconscious needs, and cultural heritage. Generally speaking, people who share similar interests are more likely to develop friendships. Before initiating a relationship, consider what it is about this person that you find attractive. Are you attracted to this person because you know that you share similar interests, in which case you have a basis for conversation? Or are you attracted to this person by some relatively superficial quality, such as looks or status, which gives you little insight into the real person?

The secret to finding someone to love is first finding someone to like. A true love relationship takes time—it's not something one jumps into lightly. Take a look inside yourself. Spend time thinking about what you really want in a relationship with another person. What things do you bring to the relationship? What do you hope to gain? It's important that we think through our dream about what makes a love relationship—then maybe it can become a reality.

27

## LOVING RELATIONSHIPS

We have all heard "You would if you loved me." This line conveys exactly what love isn't. Love is honest, understanding, and individual. Compromises may be made, but not to the point where you compromise yourself and your values.

Love can be mature and immature. Immature love is exhausting. The people involved have a hostile yet dependent relationship. Such people feel that they cannot stand to be apart and they can't stand to be together. Popular songs often depict this problem of loving someone and not being able to live without him or her. People remain in immature love situations because they feel they would be lost without the other. This type of dependency inhibits personal growth. Energy levels are low and pleasing oneself is usually more important than pleasing a partner.

A mature love relationship is stable, lasting, and open to growth. People who are in a mature love relationship have a great deal of energy and time for other activities and relationships. These experiences add to the relationship and keep the individuals interesting and interested. The time spent apart is also enjoyable, adding to one's individual growth. The partners want to please each other a little more than themselves. This can occur at any age. As love grows, trust and commitment grow. Problems are resolved with empathy and true appreciation for the other.

So when someone uses the line "You would if you loved me," remember it is just that: a line. A caring person never uses sex as a test of love.

## FAQS

1. **How do you get a shy guy to ask you out if you are shy yourself? Help! Female, Sophomore**
   *Try taking mini-steps before you try for great leaps. Maybe you and this young man are not ready for dating in a very serious way. Perhaps the place to begin is a shared conversation, studying together at the library, or simply taking a walk together. Friendship, which is the basis for most*

meaningful relationships, is built on shared experiences. Such experiences often occur in routine daily life.

2. **Almost 4 years have passed and I haven't been asked out by a female yet! On the other hand, I have asked out a few dozen women and have been turned down by all. I am average height, weight, looks, and intelligence. I have many hobbies and interests. Well, here I am. What's going wrong?!? Male, Senior**

   *I don't know. Do you have a friend that you feel close enough to? Maybe you could ask him for his opinion. One suggestion is: If you think you would enjoy knowing someone better, you may want to begin with a few minutes of shared conversation or some minor shared time together rather than a real date. If the "vibes" are good, you might want to consider something longer, like going for a walk. Before you get around to asking for a date, you should have some basis for shared experiences that allows both you and the other person to determine whether you are likely to enjoy sharing an entire evening together. The best dates are often those that start from a friendship.*

3. **I think I'm in love with a guy I met 2 weeks ago. He lives on the same floor in my dorm. What should I do? I know he likes me, too. Should I ask him out? Female, First-Year**

   *I'm wondering what you mean when you say, "in love." You've only known each other for 14 days. If you mean you find him interesting, that's nice. However, I would proceed with caution. How about starting by developing a strong friendship with him. Since he lives on your floor, you have ample opportunity to see and talk with him. My only worry is that you might rush into something you will regret later. I'd try to take it slow at first and get to know him better before asking him out on a date. Remember, no matter how your relationship develops, you'll still have to pass him in the hall at 7:00 A.M. with your bucket of shampoo and toothpaste in hand.*

4. **I've been a best friend of this girl for 2 years. I'm starting to develop stronger feelings for her now and**

**I believe she feels the same way. How do I break the ice and not ruin the friendship if things don't work out? Male, Sophomore**

*As with any relationship, a person must often take risks to move forward. Unfortunately, there are no guarantees that things will work out. However, it is helpful that you have already established a friendship. But before you talk with her about how you're feeling, I suggest you think about how you'll feel if she says she just wants to continue to be friends. Will you be able to continue the friendship? I would guess that if your friendship is important to both of you, you will be able to work things out.*

5. **Why do some women desire to sleep with someone of status—specifically a jock? Male, First-Year**

   *I believe that attraction is a complex matter. While it is possible that a woman (or a man) may wish to sleep with someone purely as a status achievement, relationships cannot be built on a single dimension any more than you would be comfortable sitting in a chair with one leg.*

6. **How can I get someone to notice me? This girl doesn't even realize I'm alive. Male, Sophomore**

   *I can imagine how frustrating it must be to be interested in someone, yet feel that the other person does not even know you are alive. I'm wondering if, when you say you want the person to notice you, you also want her to like you? As you probably already know, one cannot force another person to like (or love) you. Perhaps you could begin by finding something you both have in common to discuss. This may open the door to further conversation and eventual friendship.*

7. **I am attracted to a woman in my English class and am afraid to ask her out because I don't know if she will be attracted to me. What should I do? Female, Senior**

   *Assuming this woman is a lesbian, I suggest you find ways to get to know her a little better around class time before pursuing something outside the classroom. Arriving early, sitting next to her in class, or catching her on the way out of class may provide time to get to know her a little better and give you more information about how "available" she is in terms of dating. Should she turn down your offer for a date, please do not take it personally. She may just have other commitments or interests at this time.*

## 8. How do you know if you're in love? Male, First-Year

*My first response would be to say, "If you think you're in love, you may be." Some things to look at are: Do you care for each other to the extent that you are concerned about the other's well-being? In a loving relationship you can make adult choices that enhance both your well-being and the beloved's well-being, even though that may mean delaying gratification. In a loving relationship, for example, if you're looking to the future, you may be more serious about long-term planning and willing to forgo some of the "wild and crazy" parties and such. Small things shared together can be a delight with someone you love. At this point in the relationship you don't need a lot of money, fancy clothes, or many other people; you do need time to be together, time to share yourself, your ideals, your dreams, your innermost self. If you are both in love, you will want to be with this person most of all and will find even the most mundane, ordinary things about him or her interesting.*

## 9. How can I get an athlete to fall in love with me? Female, Junior

*Nobody can make another person fall in love with him or her. Love is a gift—not something you can negotiate.*

## 10. I used to be very much in love with my boyfriend, but I can honestly say that since we have been back at school together this semester I feel dead inside. I don't seem to have any feelings left. Is there any way I can get the feeling back? Female, Senior

*I guess that depends on what you want. Sometimes when we have experienced a number of hurts and disappointments in a relationship we "shut down" our feelings. By shutting off negative feelings, we block positive ones of love and affection as well. However, people can change their feelings, especially if they understand the causes. In your case, it may be helpful to meet with a counselor to talk about your feelings, get them out, and unfold all the things you resent in the relationship. Then you can get your partner involved and let him know the things that trouble you. If these things can be discussed openly and honestly, you may not have any more reasons to be resentful. You and your partner can start to rebuild your love for one another. Couples are often surprised by how they can change their negative feelings to positive ones once the sources of their resentment are identified and discussed, and they can then start being nice to each other again. It will not be easy at first, but it is possible.*

11. **Recently my husband and I and our two best friends, just joking around, ended up in bed. Before I knew it, I had sex with my husband's friend and my husband had sex with my friend. Although we all enjoyed it, we talked about it and realized it should never happen again. We are all mature adults and feel this won't change our friendship. Do you think this will have any long-term effects? How do you think this will affect my relationship with my husband? Female, Sophomore**

    *I cannot see that it won't change your friendship. Your letter seems to suggest, "We're all going to put our heads in the sand now and everything will be just fine." I think it will be extremely difficult to ignore the impact of this kind of activity. For starters, your wedding vows to remain faithful to one another have been broken, since this would qualify as "unfaithful," no matter how you slice it. I would expect that trust has been damaged, self-esteem has been damaged, and your relationship has been damaged. While it may not show now, it will likely show when there is pressure. For example, how do you know when he storms out during an argument that he's not seeking solace from your friend, or how can you be sure that when the four of you are together and he is alone with her in the kitchen mixing drinks that nothing is going on?*

    *I also think it's highly unlikely that all four of you were in complete agreement to participate—someone in the group may have had to be convinced or felt pressured to go along. And even if you never do it again, the questions will still be there. For example, "How was it with my best friend?" "How much did you really enjoy this?" "Was she as good as me?" "Do you wish you could do it again?" How can you take four people and assume no one will fantasize about the shuffling? I suspect it will cost something in the* relationship—there's no way you can go on being best friends and be together without these issues arising. There's a saying that may be appropriately applied to your situation: Friendship is like china—costly, rich, and rare; once damaged it can be repaired, but the crack is always there. *While I am glad that the four of you were able to talk about it, I think you and your husband also need to talk between yourselves. You and he may want to seek counseling to reestablish the validity of your relationship with each other and to rebuild the trust.*

12.  **I'm in a relationship that has lasted almost a year. I feel I am in love with my girlfriend but I am not sexually attracted to her. We have even talked about getting engaged this Christmas and I'm wondering if our relationship can last without the physical part being there. Male, Senior**

*It sounds like you have a nice friendship going with this woman. However, I don't believe you can have a long-lasting romantic relationship with someone you aren't attracted to. What is interesting is that your question is almost the reverse of what many people worry about who say, "All we have is sex, sex, sex. Is that enough of a basis for a long-term relationship?" I guess I'm wondering what you would like in a relationship. Do you wish it were different? Have you ever experienced sexual attraction to another person you were involved with? I am also concerned about why there is no attraction. How does your partner feel about this? Is she okay with the relationship as it stands? Or does she feel rejected? What are her expectations for the future? Again, I am referring to sexual attraction, not sexual activity; you can have one without the other. I think sometimes people avoid the sexual part to avoid intimacy or connection. In other words, they protect themselves by physical and emotional distance. I also wonder if part of your lack of sexual attraction for your partner concerns a fear of sex itself. Have you experienced some type of trauma or hurt feelings around sex? I think you are right to ask yourself now if this lack of sexual attraction is going to be a concern for the future. Ignoring it will not make it go away. These are just some of the issues you may want to look at with a professional. Talking with someone you can*

*trust will give you the perspective you need to make im-
portant decisions. Including your partner in these conversations will be essential. Good luck!*

13. **I'm concerned about a friend of mine who is infatuated
    with this woman in our class. He has told her his feel-
    ings for her and she said she wants nothing more than
    a friendship. She's a genuinely nice person who doesn't
    want to lead him on or hurt his feelings. Despite this, he
    talks about her 24/7, calls her constantly, and stops
    by to see her. He is starting to make an ass out of
    himself—it's embarrassing. As his friend, I feel I should
    do something, but I don't want him to get mad at me.
    Female, Sophomore**

    *Let me begin by saying that you are not responsible for
    your friend. It's not your job to protect him from making
    an "ass" of himself. He is responsible for his own behav-
    ior. I do think there is something to be said for being hon-
    est, however. For example, the next time he mentions her,
    you may want to tell him that you are uncomfortable lis-
    tening to him talk about someone who's obviously not in-
    terested in him—and leave it at that. It sounds like this is
    really between him and the woman. You say this woman
    doesn't want to hurt his feelings; yet maybe she needs to
    be more direct with him, even if it means hurting his feel-
    ings. It sounds like he didn't take the gentle "hint" that
    she's not interested—since he's constantly calling her and
    stopping by to see her. It's up to her to set limits.*

14. **I would like to have a girlfriend, someone to be in love
    with, but I seem to be a loser in the "romance de-
    partment." Any tips? Male, Junior**

    *Yes, I have a great tip: In order to find someone to love,
    you need to find someone you like. Think about what it
    says: start slow; take small steps. Rather than thinking
    you are a loser, I suspect you just have not found the right
    person yet. No one can expect to meet someone and auto-
    matically have a dynamic love relationship; it takes time.
    Begin by finding someone you like.*

15. **There's a guy at school who's been interested in me
    for several months. When he first started talking to me,**

I never considered dating him. There were no sparks whatsoever. But since there wasn't anybody else, I have gone out with him just about every weekend; but I always insist on paying my way because I don't want to give him any ideas. We do get along great, we laugh a lot and always have a good time, and I suppose I could get to like him more if I let myself. But in the past I've always known it from the first time we met when a guy was going to be my boyfriend. I would feel an instant attraction, and so would he. I feel strange letting myself become closer to this guy since the chemistry wasn't there in the first place. **Female, Junior**

*If you read your own letter carefully, you should see the answer to your question. You fell in love quickly with all of your past boyfriends, and what happened to those relationships? They didn't last. Of course that doesn't mean that a "love-at-first-sight" type of relationship can't last, only that it is not a good indication of whether or not it will. So if you find yourself slowly developing those love feelings for this guy, stop fighting it. I really support the slogan: "Start a trend, fall in love with a friend." In this way, you get to know the person first, before developing a love relationship.*

# IV

SIGNAL
AHEAD

### NORMAL SEXUAL THOUGHTS

All thoughts, feelings, wishes, desires, and fantasies, whether sexual or not, are completely normal. Everyone has probably had sexual thoughts or fantasies that others might consider perverted or unacceptable. Just because you have these thoughts does not mean something is wrong with you. As long as you realize your thoughts are normal, no matter how outrageous they are, you will not feel uncomfortable about them. All thoughts, including sexual thoughts, are normal.

### NORMAL SEXUAL BEHAVIOR

As long as sexual behavior is found enjoyable, and is acceptable to the people involved, it is okay, whatever the behavior. Behavior becomes abnormal when it is forced physically or psychologically onto another person, when it leaves feelings of guilt, and when it is generally displeasing. People who tend to engage in this type of behavior have low self-esteem and are not happy. Behavior that is willingly engaged in by adults and that does not take advantage of another person is considered normal.

## SEXUAL SELF-PLEASURING

Masturbation (playing with one's self, jerking off) is manipulation of your genitals for pleasure, also called sexual self-pleasuring. It is a normal way to express your sexuality at any age and causes no physical harm, no matter how frequently it is performed. There is no need to feel guilty about masturbating. Some people masturbate regularly, others infrequently, some not at all. How much is too much? Once a year? Once a month? Once a day? Well, it's an individual decision. The answer is once is too much if you don't feel comfortable with it. It is also too much if it is compulsive. Some men and women have their best orgasms when masturbating and many people masturbate even though they are in a sexually satisfying relationship. Masturbation is a good way to explore your own and your partner's bodies. How you masturbate or if you masturbate is your own private concern that you should not feel guilty about. Remember it's normal. If you don't like it, don't do it. But masturbation can be a substitute for and an addition to a sexually satisfying relationship.

## ORGASM

Orgasm is predominantly a psychological experience. The amount of pleasure can vary with each sexual experience and in some sexual experiences, it may not occur at all. This does not mean that the sexual experience was not enjoyed, it only means there was no orgasm.

There are too many myths surrounding the orgasm. To set the record straight, everyone is capable of achieving orgasm. Many women will never experience orgasm during intercourse. Men can ejaculate without orgasm, and it is quite rare for both partners to reach orgasm simultaneously. The best way to know what your partner finds pleasurable is to ask and to experiment. Talk openly with your partner and help each other to explore.

## FAQS

1. **I have never had sex with someone of the same sex, but have often admired their bodies. Is this unusual? Female, Sophomore**

   *No, it's not unusual. All of us can admire human bodies (both male and female) with pleasure. A trip to an art museum demonstrates that the human body has great beauty. It would be sad if one could see beauty in only half the people.*

2. **I have been seeing a woman for 3-1/2 years. This was the first sexual relationship for each of us. We are both very much in love, but here's the problem: I think about relationships with other women, specifically two other women I am friends with. I think of these women every day, and every day I feel guilty. It's driving me crazy. I often fantasize about having sex with these women, sometimes even when I am making love to my girlfriend. I can't stand the idea of hurting my girlfriend. My feelings of guilt and confusion are affecting my concentration and I often become depressed. Help! Male, Senior**

   *It's not unusual for both men and women to have sexual fantasies about others when engaged in sex. That's not something to feel guilty about. Of greater concern is the sense of conflict that emerges from your letter. Because your girlfriend is your first love and such a significant relationship, it may be difficult for you to understand that other relationships may be even better. I would suggest that you take advantage of the nearest counseling center to talk over this problem and to gain insight on yourself. I understand that you are confused and distressed by your sense of disloyalty, and I believe you can profit much by talking these matters over with an experienced counselor.*

3. **Most of my straight male friends have fantasized about watching or being with two women at the same time. I can't find even one female who has had the same fantasy about two men. Why is this? Why is that such a turn-on for men, but a turn-off for women? Female, Senior**

   *I guess you haven't asked the right women! There are women who fantasize about being with two or more men. You may want to pick up a book detailing women's sexual fantasies (e.g.,* Women on Top *by Nancy Friday)! Remember: We still live in a time when women are not really supposed to think about sex—or if they do, they should only be thinking and fantasizing about the man they love. Unlike men, women haven't been given as much freedom to explore their sexuality.*

4. **I enjoy sex with my boyfriend, but I always need to have a sex fantasy to become aroused. I never tell my boyfriend because I feel guilty that I cannot be aroused just by his touch or word. Is it normal for women to fantasize during sex? Does it mean I do not love my partner enough? My fantasy usually involves some lewd sex scene, especially rape. Is there something wrong with me? Female, Sophomore**

   *Most people have sexual fantasies. Some studies have shown that as many as 75% of us fantasize as a way of getting interested in sex or to add a little extra. The great thing about fantasy is that you are in control. The fantasy is the film and you are not only the producer, director, and scriptwriter, but also the casting director and camera operator. Fantasy allows you to run through images in your mind that give you a thrill in theory, but which you wouldn't necessarily want to experience in reality. A good example is rape. Common fantasies are making love to your partner in a romantic place, having sex with someone other than your partner, being watched, or watching others have sex. Both men and women indulge in rape fantasies. Nancy Friday, author of several books on women's fantasies (*My Secret Garden, Forbidden Flowers, *and* Women on Top)*, discusses why she feels some women fantasize about rape: "Rape does for woman's sexual* *fantasy what the first martini does for her in reality: both relieve her of responsibility and guilt. By putting herself in the hands of her fantasy assailant—by making him an assailant—she gets him to do what she wants him to do, while seeming to be forced to do what he wants. Both ways she wins, and all the while she is blameless, at the mercy of a force stronger than herself." She goes on to say that the message isn't in the plot, but in the emotions that story releases. I strongly suggest you read some of her books for reassurance (they are all available in paperback).*

5. **How important are simultaneous orgasms? Male, Sophomore**

   *Not very. In fact, "separate turns" may be even more plea-surable, especially in a new relationship where you are getting to know each other. Most people find they are un-able to fully experience their own sensations while trying to give pleasure to their partner.*

6. **Is it true that it is harder for women to achieve orgasm than men? Male, Senior**

   *I'm assuming you are referring to sexual intercourse ver-sus masturbation. Although it may take a woman longer to become aroused, she tends to stay aroused longer than a man. Awareness and consideration of individual differ-ences enhances lovemaking. Most women need stimula-tion of the clitoris. Intercourse is usually not the most effective way to get it. The vagina is too far from the clitoris for intercourse alone to provide sufficient stimulation for orgasm.*

7. **Some of the women I have slept with have not been able to reach orgasm and others have. Why is that? Male, Senior**

   *Every person is unique. What is a turn-on for one person may not be so for another. I don't believe there is a magic universal formula that leads to orgasm for every woman. You may want to explore with your partners what is satis-fying for each of them and what they desire. This may in-crease your sexual repertoire and lead you to some new discoveries about yourself as well.*

8. **How can you tell if a woman has had an orgasm? Can you tell if she is faking? Male, Junior**

   *Probably the best thing to do is ask. While one may be able to tell by the intensity of her response (e.g., breathing, muscle tension), it may not be obvious—especially if it is the first time you are together. Can a woman fake an orgasm? Yes. So can men. If you haven't seen the movie* When Harry Met Sally, *you may want to check it out. There's a great restaurant scene in which Sally addresses this issue.*

9. **I've never had an orgasm. What can I tell my boyfriend to do to accomplish one if I really don't know myself? Female, First-Year**

   *It all starts with you. I suggest you begin by familiarizing yourself with your own body. One book that has been helpful for many women in your situation is* For Each Other *by Lonnie Barbach. Her book discusses female anatomy, pleasure, and touching, as well as how to communicate your needs and desires to your partner. Every woman is unique. The only way your partner will know how to please you is if you understand yourself.*

10. **Is there any difference in feeling from an orgasm achieved by masturbation and one during intercourse or stimulation by a partner? Female, Junior**

    *Some women have reported that an orgasm achieved through masturbation is often more intense and more quickly reached because they have direct control of what feels good. An orgasm reached through stimulation by a partner may take longer to achieve, especially through intercourse—when the clitoris receives only indirect stimulation. While masturbation certainly has its benefits, some women report it lacks the emotional connectedness felt when with a partner.*

11. **Do women really fake orgasms? Male, Junior**

    *Certainly, some women have faked or do fake orgasm; so do some men. Actually, as our society has come to expect that women should be enjoying sex, the pressure for her to reach orgasm (or to pretend she has) has increased;*

*more women are probably faking now (so much for sexual freedom) than in earlier times when women's enjoyment wasn't even discussed or expected.*

## 12. What are the specifics of the phenomenon known as multiple orgasm? Male, First-Year

*It refers to experiencing more than one orgasm during a single episode of sexual activity. In fact, one of the most frequently quoted findings of Masters and Johnson (the famous sex researchers from the 1960s) is their report of multiple orgasms in many of the women they studied. This phenomenon was seen in only a few of the men they studied. Because of this, some have interpreted this to mean that women are "more sexual" than men. And, believe it or not, others have suggested that women who are multi-orgasmic are sexually superior to other women who have only one orgasm at a time. The reality is that the quality of the sexual interaction is more important than the quantity.*

## 13. Is stimulation of the clitoris the only way for a woman to have an orgasm? And what if during intercourse the clitoris doesn't get stimulated? Female, Senior

*To answer your first question, there are lots of ways women reach orgasms. Most women find stimulation of the clitoris is necessary for orgasmic response. However, some women find stimulation around the genital area or through intercourse (particularly stimulation of the G-spot inside the vagina) sufficient. Other women can reach orgasm with breast stimulation. I once knew a woman who claimed she could reach orgasm simply by having her eyebrow brushed. Some women don't even need to be touched. They can reach orgasm from fantasy or via erotic dreams.*

*In terms of your second question, when it comes to intercourse, there is often a lack of stimulation of this area (since the clitoris is hiding in the folds of skin outside and above the vaginal opening), and many women are unable to reach orgasm solely through penetration of the vagina. Most couples find it helpful to incorporate techniques for making sure the clitoris is adequately stimulated either before, during, or immediately after intercourse.*

14. **Can a woman have an orgasm in her sleep? How common is this? Female, Junior**

*Yes, orgasm can occur during sleep and is called nocturnal orgasm. When orgasm occurs, males usually notice ejaculate—hence the term wet dreams. Female orgasm may be more difficult to determine, due to the absence of such a visible sign. However, women do experience orgasm while sleeping and have woken up to incredible orgasms. While it may seem rare, studies have found upwards of 30% of women reporting that they have experienced nocturnal orgasm.*

15. **Does a man experience physical pain if he does not ejaculate (reach orgasm) while being sexually aroused? Female, Junior**

*Over the years millions of young men have used this argument to persuade young women to have sex with them. There can be discomfort for a man who is aroused and does not ejaculate, and rarely there is the pain referred to as "Lover's Nuts" or "Blue Balls." (By the way, women also experience discomfort from unrelieved arousal, referred to as "Blue Lips.") A man does not require anything from a woman to relieve his discomfort. He can take matters in hand himself or just stop doing whatever is causing the arousal. In general, the discomfort will subside after a short period of time.*

16. **Can a man successfully fake an orgasm? Male, Senior**

*Yes, a man can fake an orgasm—and many men say they have. It's sad, but true: Some people are not always honest about their experiences. Recognize that ejaculation and orgasm are two separate entities—a man can ejaculate and feel pretty bored with the experience, or he can feel like it is the most stimulating experience he has had in quite awhile. One wonders why anyone would bother to fake—why not just be honest and stop? But many people indicate it's easier to fake than to disappoint their partner by saying they are too tired or that it wasn't that great of an experience. I guess it takes time to build trust in the relationship; in this case, the trust isn't there yet.*

17. **How do you tell your partner of one year that your "great" sex together involves fake orgasms all the time? Female, Junior**

*Carefully and sincerely. And make sure this conversation happens outside the bedroom. I believe your question reflects a situation other women have found themselves in. Let me begin by saying it is important to be honest with him—he needs to know the kind of **pressure** you have felt and that your intent was never to hurt him but to "protect" him from what you thought would be disappointing. You need to have an honest talk about how you feel and how you two need to learn what does need to happen to allow you to reach orgasm. For example, he needs to be educated on the fact that most women do not reach orgasm simply from "penis-in-vagina" activity—for many women there needs to be extra stimulation. Some women even **prefer** to orgasm through manual stimulation only or oral sex or with a vibrator—not during intercourse. Please know that he's probably going to be hurt—expect that and let him be hurt. He has a right to his feelings. But you'll find that, if you can work through this, your relationship will be stronger in the long run. As you know, dishonesty makes for a very weak relationship. It's like a table with one leg—not very sturdy. Best wishes.*

18. **Friends and I were debating whether it is healthy to masturbate every day. I think one can, but they disagree. What do you think? Male, Senior**

*You are correct in thinking that a person can masturbate every day; some people do. It's important to recognize that masturbation has been a source of social concern and censure throughout history, leaving many people misinformed and feeling pretty guilty and ashamed. Many of these negative attitudes are rooted in the early Judeo-Christian view that sex was only for procreation. While today we see more positive attitudes about masturbation as a normal sexual behavior, a common concern that still exists has to do with "doing it too much." But how much is "too much"? Once a day might feel like too much to one person, while once a month might seem like too much to another. The definition of "healthy and normal" varies from person to person. A lot* depends on how the person feels about masturbation: Do they feel horribly guilty or ashamed? Does it interfere with other important tasks that need to be accomplished? One might guess that if a person were masturbating so much that it significantly interfered with schoolwork, there would be cause for concern. But, in that case, masturbation would be an indication of a problem, rather than it being the problem itself. For example, someone who is experiencing intense emotional anxiety about adjusting to college may use masturbation as an attempt to release the anxiety or as a form of self-comforting. The problem is the source of the anxiety (adjusting to college) rather than the masturbation. For most, masturbation is an ongoing love affair that each of us has with ourselves throughout our lifetime.

**19. Could a person like masturbation so much that they wouldn't ever want to have sex with a partner? Male, First-Year**

Masturbation does seem to have certain advantages over intercourse. It is simple, can be done quickly, and you don't have to worry or be concerned about catching a disease or about the desires and needs of a partner. Also, some people find the intensity of orgasm from masturbation to be greater than that of orgasms they have through sex. Regardless of all of this, most people still prefer "partner sex" as much or sometimes more than masturbation because of the many rewards partner sex provides in addition to orgasm. If a person always (not just occasionally) preferred masturbation to partner sex, it would likely be a symptom of difficulty in interpersonal relationships. The masturbation would not be the cause of the problem.

**20. Why would anyone choose to masturbate over sex? Male, Sophomore**

By sex, I am assuming you mean sexual intercourse. There are probably lots of reasons someone would choose to masturbate. For example, in an age of concern about HIV, it's the safest form of sex—free of disease. It's also a great way for women to learn how to have an orgasm; then she can tell her partner what feels good. For a man who

*ejaculates earlier than he would like when having inter-
course, he can learn to control his orgasm through masturbation. Also, some people feel they can have a stronger
orgasm through masturbation—rather than with a partner
(less distractions, plus they know what feels best for
them). If you're in a relationship where you have a higher
sexual interest than your partner, you can use masturbation to satisfy that interest, rather than feel frustrated waiting for your partner to get in the mood.*

### 21. Is it normal for a person in a relationship to mastur-
### bate? Male, First-Year

*Yes. Masturbation seems to be one of the most widely prac-
ticed and least talked about sexual behaviors. And it isn't
just "beginner's sex" that kids do until they're ready for the
"real thing." Men and women, boys and girls, people with
a regular partner and those who are single, heterosexuals and homosexuals, all masturbate. While some may believe that single adults are more likely to masturbate, the
1994 Sex in America survey found that adults with a partner are more likely to masturbate than those who did not
have a partner. The researchers concluded that masturbation is "not an outlet so much as a component of a sexually active lifestyle." Some people worry that if their
partner masturbates, there must be something wrong with
their relationship. However, there appears to be no relationship between frequency of masturbation and frequency
of sex with one's partner. If fact, some studies have found
that married people who masturbate have greater marital
and sexual satisfaction than those who do not.*

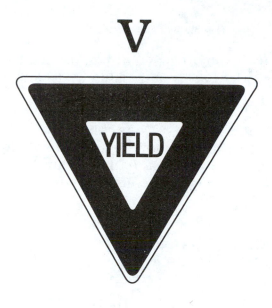

V

## DATING DILEMMAS: RELATIONSHIP IN CRISIS

Someone once said, "Happiness is not the absence of conflict, but the ability to cope with it." Sometimes people think they can meet someone in an evening, fall in love, and that's it—a love relationship has been established. But it needs to be based on something, such as mutual interests or values. It also has to be based on compromise. In any relationship, there are differences that need to be worked out. You may find yourself struggling in a relationship with any number of issues: commitment, monogamy, expectations, communication, jealousy, or long-distance dating.

While it is not possible to change another person, you can modify things a bit. By talking directly to your partner, you can try to help him or her understand that you have certain needs and desires. It is up to your partner to hear this and respond. To help the other person hear your concerns, you'll need to speak clearly, in the context of "I care about our relationship," and with specifics. Sometimes we have to move out of the "comfort zone" and take risks. Recognize that you have to work at any relationship. It doesn't just happen.

If, after expressing your needs and desires, you find no change or consideration for what you have stated, you should ask yourself a few things: Does this relationship feel "balanced"? Do I get enough from this relationship in other ways to continue in it? How much of myself am I willing to compromise? Why am I willing to stay in a relationship that ignores my desires?

# FAQS

1.  **I have a problem. My boyfriend and I have been going out for a year. A lot of the time he treats me as if my feelings don't matter and often puts me down for saying things that he doesn't feel are important. I love him very much, so I don't want to say anything to him about this. My friends are encouraging me to stand up for myself, but I don't dare to because he yells at me when he gets mad. This upsets me greatly. Our sex life is wonderful, except that most of the time he gets so excited that he comes almost instantly. I have never had an orgasm, but I think maybe I could if he would last longer. I hesitate to tell him any of this because he assumes that he is a wonderful lover. He tends to get offended and defensive when I offer constructive criticism. What do I do? What do I say to him? Female, Sophomore**

    *Are you staying with this man because you like to be kicked or because you are afraid you can't find someone better? As you describe this relationship, I find it difficult to imagine what satisfactions and joys there can be for you in this. You are entitled to have someone treat you with respect and caring. A good relationship is a relationship of equals—both of whom care about and seek the well-being of the other. The relationship you describe sounds very much like exploitation, in which you are doing all the caring, nurturing, giving, and loving and receiving nothing positive in return. You may want to consider ending this* relationship and seeking one that is more positive for you. One word of advice: If you continue to find yourself in this kind of destructive relationship, you may want to consider making an appointment with a counselor.

2. **I just found out that the person I've been seeing since last semester has a boyfriend at home. She hasn't told me; I found out from her roommate. How do I handle this? Male, Sophomore**

   *There seem to be some unknowns: (1) You don't know how serious her relationship at home is; it could be a childhood sweetheart or just a close friend. (2) I don't know how serious you are about this relationship. What does this relationship mean to you? Is this a casual dating relationship or someone you see as a potential lifelong partner? Even though you are feeling hurt, it seems to me the place to begin is to sit down and talk to her. Remember: Her roommate may not have all the facts straight. You might say, "I'm feeling hurt. I understand you have a boyfriend at home and I need to know where I stand." There are many questions only she will be able to answer.*

3. **There is a woman who likes me as "more than a friend" who I would like to keep as "just a friend." How can I tell her without hurting her? Male, Senior**

   *You may not be able to save her from hurt. She is responsible for her feelings. If you are able to talk with her directly, I might suggest starting by expressing how important her friendship is to you. Emphasize what you like about her and what makes her an important friend. If she can hear that, she may be able to hear you when you explain that you would like to keep the friendship platonic. If you don't talk to her about the situation, but instead choose to let the tension continue, at some point she may feel led on. Talking to her and being honest **now** will save her (and you) a bigger hurt down the road.*

4. **I have recently started dating a guy that I have been friends with for about a year. As a friend, I had explained to him that after a very painful breakup of my last relationship, I wanted to go slowly in establishing a new relationship with someone else. He said he**

understood completely. The problem is, now that we have begun dating each other, everything I thought we discussed about going slow is out the window. He calls me a lot, asks me out two to three times a week, and if I'm not home, he jokingly wants to know what I was doing. I do like him a lot and enjoy his company; I even feel comfortable kissing him, but at this point that is all. I feel that if things keep going as they have been, it will get out of hand: What could be a good relationship will end just because it is going too fast, too soon. How should I handle this situation? I hate to use the old cliché, but I do need some "space" until I know just how I feel about him. Is there a way to go about it without hurting him? Female, Senior

*It sounds like you're feeling "smothered" by your friend. It also sounds like you need more time to recover from your last relationship before you enter a new one. In addition, it sounds like it's time to have a heart-to-heart talk with your friend. Unfortunately, it may be hard for him to hear you say how you are feeling. But in the long run it will be easier for him to accept your honesty now, rather than being "strung along" until you're to the point where you can't stand to be around him. Hopefully, he will be able to accept your feelings and understand that you need more space as well as his supportive friendship.*

5.  **I'm in my first serious relationship, but it seems we're constantly arguing. Is fighting necessarily a sign of a troubled relationship? Male, Sophomore**

    *It depends on what you're fighting about. Are you having challenging and healthy discussions about your thoughts and feelings? Are you hearing each other and respecting each other's thoughts, feelings, and opinions? In any relationship, there are disagreements and differences of opinion. That's what makes relationships interesting and fun. Arguments aren't always a sign of a bad relationship; lots of times people find out about each other through spirited discussion. What matters, I suppose, is what happens when you finish the argument. Are you able to agree to disagree? Are you still friends?*

*I hope you find time to do other things besides fight. If, however, all you do is fight—disagree and end up mad at each other—it may be time to ask yourself some questions: Why are you fighting? What are you gaining from this relationship? Do you feel better or worse about yourself after spending time together? Do you want to understand your partner or just tell her how you feel and leave it at that? Are there real differences of opinion with no room for compromise? Are you really happy? Again, I would want to know if your relationship involves more than fighting and disagreeing. Do you share fun times? Do you find time to enjoy each other? Are you happy and energized by being with this person? A healthy relationship is one that leaves you feeling better about yourself, not worse.*

6. **The guy I'm seeing is getting too emotionally involved too soon in our relationship. What can I do or say to him to get him to back off? Female, Sophomore**

*I'm not sure I understand you. What I think you're saying is you want a casual relationship and he wants a commitment. If this is so, then you need to be straight with him about your feelings. One way to cope is to say, "I like you very much and I am not ready for an exclusive relationship with you. I'd love to share a friendship with you and I also want to be with others, to meet and date other guys." It is no kindness to let a person believe that you are making a similarly total commitment to him, when in reality you're not ready to do so.*

7. **My boyfriend is afraid of getting close to me. He doesn't tell me but I *know*. He keeps the wall built up and is very insecure. How can I help to reassure him how much I care? I tell him over and over, but he finds some reason to say I do not care. Female, Junior**

*Beyond telling your boyfriend that you care, I'm not really sure what you can do to convince him. He needs to believe it himself—you can't make him believe you. Unfortunately, he may not be ready to hear what you are saying. He may not feel that he is worthy of your care and concern. I suggest you take a step back and look at your relationship. Are you willing to be involved with someone who does not embrace your feelings? Is he capable of being emotionally connected to you? Does he feel good enough about him-self? He may not be ready or mature enough to establish a relationship with another person. It's hard to have a re-lationship with a wall.*

8.  **Since the start of the semester I've developed a close friendship with this guy. It seems we do everything together—hanging out, talking 'til all hours of the night, going places together as a couple (everything from parties to church). Many people assume we are dating. We've never done anything romantic together, but I have been wondering where this will lead. Well, he told me yesterday that he doesn't want to be any-thing more than friends. Ouch! Now what do I do? Fe-male, First-Year**

    *Like many relationships, it sounds like when you two met you really "hit it off"; gradually, more and more of your free time seemed to revolve around each other. Now you've reached the next stage, where one or both people step back and say, "But, I'm an individual. How does this relation-ship fit in? How do we define ourselves?" That's what yes-terday seems to be about. I would let him know that you understand he wants a friendship. And that you do, too. You also recognize that on a certain level you had ques-tions about what your relationship meant to him and to you, where it was going, and if it would lead to other things down the road. You were unclear about what his feelings were toward you. Now that you understand, you need to ask yourself if you are willing to continue this friendship if this is all there is.*

    *It sounds like he wants all the symbol without the substance. In your world, where you spend so much time together and share so much of yourself, things progress; in his world, he says no way. He wants a friendship that has limits, which he doesn't want to see progress into anything else. He seems to want a relationship with brakes. If you are willing to continue the friendship knowing his limits, you need to make it emotionally safe for yourself. That means setting up parameters. You need to clarify who you are and what you feel comfortable doing with a friend. For example, you might specify that you're not comfortable doing things as a couple that add to the community's perception that you are more than just friends. It's perfectly all right to put limits on this, to pull back and see if the relationship holds—so it is clear to both of you and to others that you are just friends. Besides, how are you ever going to meet anyone else if you spend all your time with this guy? When the two of you are on more solid ground, you can see what happens and where you might want to move from there. The unfortunate reality is that no relationship can stay the same; any relationship that does not progress is dying.*

*Finally, if you did have hopes or expectations that this would develop into a real love relationship, it's also very important that you grieve the death of that dream so that you can move on. Best wishes.*

9. **I want to be able to date others while at college, but I have a girlfriend back home. She doesn't want to break up. Should I just go ahead and date people here and not tell my girlfriend? Male, First-Year**

*It sounds like you need to decide what you really want in relationships with others. It's difficult to have a relationship built on deception—with either your girlfriend at home or the women you would like to date at college. If you really want to date other women, you need to be honest about your feelings and tell your current girlfriend. In the long run, you won't be doing her (or you) any favors by being dishonest.*

10. **I've been sort of seeing this guy for a while. I had been seeing him last year, but we decided to break it off for the summer. I hadn't planned on seeing him this year as anything other than friends. But when I first saw him in September, I was still attracted to him. I wouldn't even classify our relationship as dating—we just have sex. That's not at all what I want. I tried talking to him a little last year about what I wanted but it didn't do any good. It's either his way or no way. I'm almost positive that all he wants is sex, but I want something more. Lately I've been thinking a lot about my past relationships and I've been feeling very regretful. I don't know what to do. Female, Junior**

*As you describe this relationship, I find it difficult to imag-ine what real satisfactions and joys there can be for you in this. You say, "It's either his way or no way," indicating your relationship is on his terms only. What about your terms? You also state, "That's not at all what I want." So why continue the relationship? How about making **you** a priority? The relationship you describe sounds very super-ficial. It sounds like you're looking for something different—a relationship with some depth or real intimacy—and you're not finding it in this one. You may want to consider ending this relationship and seeking one that is more in line with your own interests and desires. Before entering a new re-lationship, I would suggest you spend some time thinking about what you really want in a relationship with another person. It's important that you think through your dream about what makes a love relationship—then maybe it can become a reality.*

11. **I am seeing a man 21 years older than I am—he's 40 and I'm 19. He's also married but isn't in love with his wife. They are going through marriage counseling be-cause she found out about us a year ago. We started our relationship over the summer again. He says he'll know by next summer if he is going to stay married or not. Should I wait or should I just move on? Female, Sophomore**
    *This may be difficult to hear, but you should know that most men in this situation don't end up leaving their wife; if they do, they end up going back to her. I'm curious about what you see in him. He's married, he's 21 years older, he's not able to make clear decisions about relationships, and by having an affair he hasn't been honest with his wife. What attracts you to him? What are your hopes and dreams for a relationship? I think it's important that you look at your motivation for such a relationship. Can you talk to a counselor about this?*

12. **A couple of weeks ago I had a threesome with my girl-friend and one of her friends. Now, when my girlfriend and I are intimate, just the two of us, I am no longer satisfied. How do I go about telling her that I need more? Male, Senior**

In terms of threesomes, occasionally a person gets a partner to comply or go along with something like this, but not
many relationships survive. It sounds to me like you are
more intent on the sexual game than on the relationship.
I'm interested in knowing how much you care about your
partner if she says she doesn't care to participate again.
My concern has to do with one person imposing demands
on another. I'm wondering if she really wanted to participate in this threesome or if she simply went along with
your wishes. It sounds like maybe she was willing to participate that one time, but it wasn't something she necessarily wanted or wants to continue. Certainly there are
societies where threesomes exist. How would you feel
about your partner having two men? Also, how are you to
expect your girlfriend to believe you care about her if you're
saying you prefer diversity? There's a difference between
using someone for a sexual adventure and a deep meaningful relationship. Which do you want? If you want a relationship, it needs to be based on a commitment—versus
viewing her as some kind of convenient port of call.

**13. What causes people to cheat? Is it possible to have a
successful relationship with a person who has cheated
on you? Male, Sophomore**

The reasons people "cheat" (a.k.a., have an affair, commit
adultery) are varied and complex. Sometimes such relationships are motivated by a desire for excitement and variety. Some people may be motivated to gain evidence that
they are still desirable to others. In other cases people may
be unhappy with their current relationship. If emotional
needs aren't being met in the relationship, having an affair
may seem inviting. In some cases, affairs may provide just
the impetus a person needs to end a relationship they no
longer wish to be a part of. And sometimes the reason for
outside involvements may be the unavailability of sex within the relationship (e.g., due to a lengthy separation, ill-
ness, or unwillingness of the partner to relate sexually). A
person may also be motivated to cheat by a desire for
revenge.

As you might imagine, the effects of cheating can vary.
When the secret is discovered, the betrayed person
may feel devastated, or overwhelmed by feelings of

*inadequacy, rejection, extreme anger, resentment, shame, and jealousy. It is important to know that while relationships in which a partner cheats frequently end, it is possible for some couples to have a successful relationship. Sometimes, the discovery motivates a couple to search for sources of the problems within their relationship, a process that may actually lead to an improved relationship. If both partners are willing to make a commitment to the relationship, it is possible to rebuild the foundation. Trust and honesty are key components for a successful relationship. It takes time.*

**14. How do I deal with my boyfriend who has had many past relationships and keeps talking about them and how great they were? Female, Junior**

*This guy may not realize what message he is sending. He may need to be told that this is bothering you. Remind him that many people do not like to be compared to others, particularly to previous boyfriends or girlfriends. I wouldn't wait until he does it again; I would try to bring it up as soon as possible, over a casual lunch or get-together. Talk about how it makes you feel when he says these things. You may also want to ask him why he is telling you. Is it because he feels insecure and wants you to know that he has had great relationships in the past? Or is it because he is trying to drop hints about the way he would like to see his current relationship with you? Either way, he needs to know how it makes you feel. Hopefully, he will respect your feelings. However, if you tell him and he continues to share his stories, you may want to consider looking elsewhere for a more sensitive or respectful partner. There are many guys out there who are sensitive and caring and who would be respectful of your feelings.*

**15. My boyfriend gets upset when I don't want to have sex. We've been together for 2 years now. He always assumes that he's not good enough when I say no. How do I make him understand that it's not him? Female, Junior**

*You may not be able to. This guy sounds like he needs to grow up a bit. You seem to be saying that when you tell him you're not interested, he lays a guilt trip on you. I hope that you two will consider sitting down with a counselor to talk through your feelings. It sounds like he needs to learn to accept your feelings as legitimate and not necessarily see this as a rejection of him. You may also need to learn how to turn down his offer of intimacy without implying that it is about him. Good luck.*

16. **Why does my friend stay in a bad relationship that she recognizes is bad? Male, Senior**

    *Maybe it's because of her history: that is what she is most comfortable with. She may be able to find a good relationship with the help of counseling. As her concerned friend, you can discuss this with her. Be honest about what you see happening to her—what you see as a "bad relationship"—and encourage her to seek help. In other words, maybe you could point her in a different direction, recognizing that only she can actually change the direction of her life.*

17. **I think one of my friends is cheating on his girlfriend. She goes to another school and is only up here on some weekends. When she isn't around, this other girl is always tagging along with my friend. I don't know whether or not I should tell his girlfriend. I am really good friends with both of them and I don't want either of them to get hurt or get mad at me. Should I just let it be and hope it works itself out? Female, Junior**

    *There seem to be a few things you are not sure about. For example, you don't know how serious his relationship with this girl is (she "tags along"), and you don't know the "inside scoop" about his long-distance relationship, in terms of what they have decided about relationships while apart. It seems you are basing your concern on assumptions and what you are seeing. This is really between your friend and his long-distance girlfriend. If you are really good friends with both of them, and you **know for sure that he is cheating**, only then would I suggest you tell your friend that he is putting you in an awkward position. He needs to know that should his girlfriend ever ask, you are not planning to lie. In the meantime, I would not offer information to your female friend—especially as it is based on speculation at this point. Please know that you may be in* *a no-win situation if it's true that he's cheating. You may lose one of them as a friend. Brace yourself.*

**18. I have this thing I do whenever I date someone. It's like a game. I always want some kind of reassurance that I am attractive and lovable. I seem to need proof that the guys I date really care for me and want to make me happy. Sometimes I create little "tests" for them, just so I can feel confident that they really do care. Is this normal? Female, Junior**

*I think that we all look for indications that the person we are seeing cares about us. However, dating is not supposed to be a game—it requires honest and direct communication. What you're doing doesn't sound "normal" in a healthy dating relationship. I would guess that any guy you date is going to realize that you are testing him, and while he may try to pass the first few tests, eventually he is going to get tired of this game and move on. I would suggest you talk to someone about your own issues of needing reassurance. Learning to find the confidence within yourself—rather than depending on someone else—will be a useful tool for dealing with many of life's situations.*

**19. I am a very jealous guy. When I am dating someone I want to be the only thing she needs. I can't stand the thought that she might find someone else attractive or interesting. Almost always, there's no reason for me to think this way, but I can't help it. I end up driving her away. What now? Male, Sophomore**

*Hey, we all feel a bit protective of the person we love, but what you describe is somewhat extreme. As you have found out in your past relationships, this can be very destructive. You end up suffocating the person you're seeing and driving her away. So what's really going on? Do you really want the relationship to end? Are you so insecure with yourself that you have to hold on so tight to another person? I think an honest look inward will be very useful. Working to change your destructive behavior will be to your advantage. Perhaps you should talk to a counselor about this.*

**20. I'm seeing a guy from home and I have a boyfriend here at school. Neither one knows about the other. What should I do? Female, Junior**

*It's real difficult to have a deep and meaningful relationship built on a major lie. An omission of a truth as important as this is deception. If you truly care about these guys, then you need to sort out which one matters to you more, if that's the case, or whether or not you're ready for a single committed relationship. If you cannot sort out which one is more important, you probably are not ready for a committed relationship. In either case, your concern and respect for these friends should provide a basis for more open honesty on your part.*

**21. I like this woman and would like to get to know her. However, my plans for the spring semester are up in the air. I could be here or I could be living out of state. I know long-distance relationships are tough. How do I approach this? Male, Senior**

*I'm sure you've heard the phrase, "There's no time like the present." In terms of building any relationship, a person must often take risks. Why don't you try focusing on getting to know her this semester? Remember: While long-distance relationships can be tough, some of the best ones are based on a solid foundation of friendship, which you could be building with her now.*

**22. I'm in a long-distance dating relationship and I'm frustrated. Because of the distance we don't see each other very often, so we rely on the telephone. Lately the pattern is: He says he'll call and he doesn't. If I tell him it hurts my feelings and I feel forgotten, he blames me. I'm confused about what to do. Female, Senior**

*You say he blames you when you have doubts about the relationship, instead of reassuring you. Well, recognize that blame is often used to get oneself off the hook. Maybe he doesn't want the kind of relationship that involves commitment. If that's so, all the wishing in the world isn't going to bring about a commitment. It's not good to hold on to a fairy tale. It's better to find out now, rather than two years from now.*

*Why don't you give him the distance he seems to want and let him make the next move? If and when he calls, be glad to hear from him, be pleasant (e.g., "It's always nice to hear from you"), but be brief. Try not to be hostile or act hurt. See if he makes an effort. Do not pursue him. If he wants the relationship, he can come after it. Maybe he wants out because he doesn't want to be pursued, or maybe he wants out because he doesn't feel the two of you are a good match. You won't know unless you give him room to find out. While your first response may be to run/leave because you feel threatened, I suggest you walk slowly. It may be useful to sit back and play the "shrinking violet." Assess if the relationship is going anywhere. Leave him lots of room. The ball is in his court now—see if he does anything with it. View this as a learning experience. Should he not respond and the relationship fizzles out over time, think of the motto medical interns learn in surgery: Forgive and Remember. In the meantime, do something constructive for you, take care of yourself. Best wishes.*

23. **I have been seeing someone almost all semester. However, the semester break is fast approaching. I'm graduating and moving out of state and she'll be returning to college. We won't be able to see each other very much and summer seems like years away. How do I deal with a long-distance relationship? Male, Senior**
    *While long-distance relationships can be tough, they are not impossible. I think it is important to be aware of some of the issues that may arise for the two of you over the next semester and spend time together discussing them now. For example, how often do you plan to see each other, what do you plan to do when you get together, and how will you deal with extra expenses such as phone bills and travel? Forewarned is forearmed.*

24. **My boyfriend is going to another school that is pretty far away so I only get to see him on the weekends. When we have sex, he gets really tired very easily. I was wondering if it was because he hasn't had sex in a long time or if it was because he is cheating on me? Female, Junior**

*I guess the place to begin is to ask him directly. It could be he is just tired. However, if it's not "tired" that you're sensing, but instead it seems to be a lack of interest or enthusiasm, I would recommend a serious discussion with him about how you're feeling and how he's feeling. Perhaps there is some other stress in his life, maybe he's just preoccupied with school, or perhaps he has questions about your relationship. Then again, he may just be tired. What seems clear from your note is that you sense something has changed, and you see it played out in your sex life. It also sounds like you need answers and reassurance from him that it's nothing serious. You're right to follow your "gut feelings" and question if there is a problem in the relationship! Best wishes.*

**25. What do you do if you carry strong feelings for an ex-lover, but you have lost contact due to distance? I'm afraid she may be mad because I haven't called, but it was too hard to hear her voice. Can you make any suggestion of how to open the relationship again? Male, Junior**

*I would suggest writing her a letter rather than calling her. That way she isn't put on the spot or taken by surprise. It gives her the chance to think about what has happened and decide how she wants to respond. Since you say she may be mad, I would suggest including an explanation of why you haven't called (that it was too hard to hear her voice). You might also explain your current interest in reconnecting with her. Is it to rekindle a love relationship, to develop a friendship, or to just check out if she's alive? You don't indicate how long ago you were involved with her. Please be prepared to hear that she may have "moved on." She may not share your feelings. She may even be involved in another relationship. It does sound like you need some type of "closure." I hope you can find it with your letter. Good luck!*

**26. I am wondering if you have any words of advice for a long-distance relationship. We have been together for 7 months. Sometimes I feel like I am not in love just because she is not here. But when I am with her, I couldn't ask for anything more. I also feel bad if I hit on other girls. Male, Junior**

*Actually, I would really like to know more about your re-
lationship. For example, how long have you been in this
long-distance arrangement (of the 7 months you've been
dating) and when will it end so that you will be together
daily? That information might shed some light on what's
going on for you two. If this is a temporary situation (just
this semester) and then you're back together, it may be
something to hang in there for. However, if this is the way
your relationship is going to be for the next few years, you
may want to reconsider your commitment.*

*You say you are hitting on other girls. This should be
a clear indication that this long-distance relationship may
not be exactly what you had hoped for. Consider what you
want the long-distance relationship to be: just a casual one
or a serious monogamous commitment. I believe it's going
to take some soul searching—and a few conversations with
her—to figure it out.*

**27. I broke up with my boyfriend over a year ago, but I
can't stop thinking about him. I've dated other guys,
but nobody seriously. Will I ever get over him? Female,
Junior**

*Probably. One year isn't really a long time to still be think-
ing about your old boyfriend, especially when you haven't
established another serious relationship. It's important to
look at why you still think about him. Is it the relationship
with **him** that you miss, or just having **a** relationship? Why
did you break up? Often it can be easier to remember the
good times with your boyfriend, while forgetting why the
relationship didn't work out. Remember: One of our tasks
in life is learning to let go. It's hard.*

**28. I just don't get it. My boyfriend just dumped me—on
the night before our 7-month anniversary no less! I
loved him so much—I literally did everything for him.
Why can't he see how great he had it with me? I gave
him everything. I'm so mad! Now look: What did I get
in return? Nothing! Female, Sophomore**

*Please remember that there are no guarantees in relation-
ships. While we may hope that a relationship will last, it
may not. I am somewhat concerned about how you
are defining love. Let me just say that love is not about*

*significant self-sacrifice, or specifically, love is not mar-
tyring. That's what it sounds like your relationship was
about. You say you gave him everything or at least more
than you received in return. While you may have had good
intentions, it sounds like you believe that loving is doing un-
selfishly for your partner without ever being concerned
with your own needs. A martyr is just that: someone who
does more for the relationship—or feels that they do—than
do their partners. Although it sounds noble, a person who
is in the role of martyr tends to grow angry and slowly
build resentment that the relationship is not balanced. You
have a right to be angry. You did not get the return you
were looking for. However, you learned a valuable lesson
to take with you into future relationships, that is: Your
needs are as important as your partner's. Next time you
are in a love relationship, make sure things are fair and
balanced and as equal as possible—make sure you are
getting back as much as you are giving to the relationship.
You deserve it! Don't let anyone tell you that you don't!*

29. **Help! I've been in a relationship on and off for 1½ years.
Every time we go out for a while, my "friend" decides
he's not ready for a relationship. What should I do? He
does say he is attracted to me and we're best friends.
Female, Senior**

*What should you do? **Move on** to someone else if you are
interested in having a real love relationship. Certainly you
should continue to enjoy the friendship you have, but recognize that that is all it is—a friendship. As you recognize,
a platonic friendship is nice, but can only go so far, in terms
of the intimacy. It sounds like you've spent a lot of time in-
vesting in the relationship with the hopes that it could be
more than a friendship—but that has not happened. He
says he's not ready for a relationship, so believe him. And
try to stay firm on your friendship—rather than being in
an "on-again–off-again" cycle, that would only add to the
confusion (and hurt). I'm also curious why you went back
to him each time? Why didn't you believe him the first time
he told you he wasn't ready for a relationship? I feel that's
an important piece to look at. Understanding that will help
you keep the boundaries between you.*

# VI

## FIGURING OUT (AND TALKING ABOUT) SEXUAL DESIRES

Sexual communication is both an important and necessary aspect of any relationship. Couples who explore each other's needs and desires enhance the satisfaction experienced in an intimate relationship. However, many couples choose to overlook the possibilities that open communication implies. Lack of or ineffective communication is a leading cause of sexual dysfunction.

Talking about sex is not always easy, but it is necessary. Communication not only alleviates anxiety, but also heightens sexual pleasure. One might start by asking, "What do you like?" or "What feels good to you?" The bedroom may not be the best place to start this conversation. Once discussion has been started, it will be easier to talk about more sensitive topics. No matter how close your relationship may be, do not assume that your partner is a "mind reader." Although communication is sometimes difficult, it is essential to a healthy and growing relationship.

## SEX UNDER THE INFLUENCE: ALCOHOL AND OTHER DRUGS

Alcohol is probably the best-known and most widely used drug. In Shakespeare's *Macbeth*, a character asks what drinking causes and the porter replies, "It provokes the desire but takes away the performance." In small amounts alcohol reduces sexual inhibitions, but in large amounts it leads to erection problems in men and lack of orgasm in women. Even a small amount can lead to temporary dysfunction. Many a partygoer has been dismayed to find his or her performance less than usual after an evening of heavy drinking. On a more serious note, when someone has been drinking, and especially when both partners have been drinking, communication and safer sex practices tend to "go out the window." With so many serious sexually transmitted diseases today, that's a high price to pay for having sex when you're drunk.

In addition to alcohol, other drugs have been known to affect one's sexuality—and not always in a positive way. Marijuana has been reported to enhance a sexual experience by relaxing the user. Amphetamines and cocaine both have a reputation as a stimulant. While small doses might increase one's responsiveness to sex, high doses have been shown to have very negative effects on sexual functioning and can possibly lead to very negative consequences. As with alcohol, people under the influence of drugs tend to put themselves at risk for unprotected sex, and the possibility of unwanted pregnancy and disease. Finally, while using alcohol and other drugs may reduce inhibitions, it prevents you from learning how to handle sexuality in a responsible way.

## FAQS

1. **Are most women just as horny as men? Male, Junior**
   *To put it simply, yes. However, there's no one rule for everybody. While society may try to portray women as uninterested participants in sex, the reality is that people vary. Some women and some men have very high sex drives, while other men and women do not.*

2. **Is it possible to become sexually aroused and/or have an orgasm while under the influence of alcohol? Male, Junior**

   *Yes, it is possible. But keep in mind that most drugs, including alcohol, numb sexual feelings and depress sexual function unless used in very small amounts. Alcohol may loosen inhibitions or tensions to make intimacy more approachable, but at the same time may diminish physical awareness and make orgasm unlikely.*

3. **Can being in good physical condition increase your desire to have sex? Male, Senior**

   *Yes, being fit may indeed increase one's desire. There are many positive benefits to being in good physical condition. Feeling fit helps us feel better about a lot of things. We often feel better about ourselves when we think we look our best. Being in good shape often leads to positive feelings about life; our desire for many things increases.*

4. **What can I do when I want to make love, but my partner isn't "in the mood"? How can I get him in the mood? Female, First-Year**

   *Loving relationships thrive on mutual respect. I am not sure that you can make anybody feel romantic and sexy just because that's the time you're feeling romantic and sexy. Generally, "turn-ons" for men include caring, touch, warm shared feelings, and the interest in mutual respect.*

5. **I am in love with someone, but I am not sexually attracted to him. However, I am sexually attracted to other people. What do I do? Female, Junior**

   *What do you want to do? It sounds to me like you may have a fine platonic relationship. This is someone you enjoy being with, but you do not share sexual experiences. How does the man feel about this? Is it something he is happy with? I believe men and women can share friendships that are not sexual, although I think this is relatively rare. I suggest you sit down together and discuss the relationship openly and see if you are in agreement.*

6. **Is it possible for someone not to like sex and never want to participate in it again? Female, First-Year**

*Possibly. Barring a physical problem that makes sex diffi-cult or even unwelcome, not every lover is good, positive, and wonderful. Sometimes sex is hurried. Sometimes one person's needs are imposed on another whether they're ready or not. Not every partner is understanding, patient, and considerate. While one experience (or several) wasn't good, it doesn't mean you'll never enjoy sex. It might mean you just weren't with the right person, or maybe you were with the right person but you need to talk over your readi-ness and needs.*

7. **What do I do if my boyfriend isn't interested in sex? He also doesn't like to talk about sex. Female, Junior**

   *This is a serious problem, one that can ruin a relationship. You need to get him to talk. You might say, "Honey, this is real serious. We have to deal with this. Our relationship is in trouble." If he still refuses to talk about it, you'll have to think about your own needs and options. For example, is it worth it to have an affair? Break up? Will he go with you to see a counselor? Even if he refuses to go along, you may want to make an appointment to talk with someone about how you can deal with this. Good luck.*

8. **How can I tell if a woman is physically ready to have intercourse? Male, Sophomore**

   *Women's bodies usually signal readiness with lubrication, pelvic motion, and greater intensity. Many women feel com-fortable telling their partner when they are ready. If you're not sure, gently ask your partner to tell you when she is ready.*

9. **How can you keep the excitement in a relationship you've been in for some time? Won't it get stale after a while? Female, Senior**

   *This is a typical question from couples who have been to-gether for years. Anything that is routine, that happens over and over again in the same exact way, becomes bor-ing or stale. Even sex. For many couples, sex becomes a routine that is performed at the end of the day, when you're both exhausted, just before falling asleep. How can you spice up the relationship? Make things different: change your positions, places, and times; add little sur-prises; do the things that used to turn you on, which have now fallen to the side. It's important to find ways to vary your experiences—this means communicating and negotiating with your partner.*

**10. As strange as this may sound, I can't understand how or why my boyfriend likes my breasts. He says they turn him on, but I guess I don't feel confident or something. Female, First-Year**

*When it comes to concerns about breast size, I think it's similar to some people's concerns about penis size:* It's a bigger issue in the locker room than it is the bedroom. *Too often we think breasts come in only two sizes: too big or too small. With all the messages from the media about "perfect" bodies, it's not surprising that you (and some other women) feel uncomfortable with your breast size. Let me point out, there may be many reasons your partner enjoys your breasts. Size is only one factor to consider, and it is irrelevant for many couples. Maybe he likes the way your breasts look, feel, taste, and smell. Maybe he likes their texture, shape, or design. Maybe he likes them because they are part of you.*

**11. What do you do if you're not in the mood but your partner is? Female, Sophomore**

*Follow your instincts. You're not in the mood, so tell your partner. Talk about it. Maybe after some discussion you'll change your mind, and maybe not. One hopes you have the kind of mutual respect in your relationship to allow for such differences of opinion, interests, and perspectives.*

**12. Are there certain foods that stimulate sex or sexual desire? I think so, but maybe that's just me. Male, Sophomore**

*It's true that some foods and chemicals have been alleged to act as sexual stimulants for those who consume them. These are called* aphrodisiacs. *A wide variety of substances have been labeled aphrodisiacs, including powdered rhinoceros's horn, powdered stag's horn, dried salamanders, and dried beetles (just the thought of ingesting such things makes me lose interest!), along with some foods such as eggs, olives, peanuts, oysters, venison, and bananas. While research would suggest that there are no real aphrodisiacs, it is probably true that so-called aphrodisiacs work because the user believes in their effectiveness. Some researchers have said that one of the most effective aphrodisiacs is an interesting and expressively interested partner.*

13. **My boyfriend's idea of foreplay is touching and fondling. My idea of foreplay is having a nice conversation first—that's what turns me on! The problem is that we can never do it my way. Why is it so hard for him to realize that I really *can* get turned on with a nice conversation?! Female, Sophomore**

*Someone once told me: "Men look for a place, women look for a reason," suggesting that when it comes to sex men and women are worlds apart. Your situation sort of fits here. It will be important to have an honest discussion with your partner about your differences. What concerns me about your question is the sense that sex is his way or no way. What happens in this type of situation is that resentment begins to build. If this relationship is going to proceed in a healthy direction, you need to establish ground rules you can both live with. In a loving relationship there is concern for the other and a sense of balance. He really does need to accept that the two of you have different ways of responding sexually, and have respect for that part of you that is unique. Hopefully he will realize that, in the long run, it is in his interest as well as yours to incorporate your feelings and desires, knowing that this will lead to a healthier and happier relationship.*

14. **Why do I like to videotape myself? Male, First-Year**

*I'm not sure . . . probably because you like what you're seeing on the monitor. It seems to be the latest rave—now that more and more people have access to home camcorders. It's certainly less expensive than renting a video and watching strangers. This way you know exactly what you're going to see. Just be careful about who gets their hands on your home movies!*

15. **I have a problem. I think I come too fast. My girlfriend has never said anything, but I think I do. What should I do? Male, Senior**

*Too fast for what? It used to be thought that a man came "too fast" if he came before his partner. Now we know that most women don't reach orgasm from simple intercourse.*

*So . . . too fast for what? Sex shouldn't include a stopwatch. If your partner hasn't said anything, maybe you should ask her. She may not agree. However, one suggestion is you may want to try to expand your definition of sex, thinking of it as more than just intercourse. Certainly slowing things down, focusing less on reaching orgasm and more on the pleasure of giving, will help.*

16. **I'm in a relationship that means a great deal to me. Every aspect is almost perfect, except sex. Whenever we have sex, I feel like he always has an orgasm and I do not. Sometimes I feel we're not sexually compatible. Is this normal? Female, Sophomore**

*I guess I am concerned about your interaction in the bedroom; what happens there often reflects upon the relationship. I don't know, but maybe your partner doesn't understand some basic things about pleasuring you. Have you talked with him about your desire to reach orgasm too? How aware is he of the problem? Is he just inexperienced and doesn't realize sex is for mutual pleasuring—not just his? If this is the case, a little reading and talking can solve your problem. However, if he is fully aware of the situation and just doesn't care, you have a much more serious problem. If this is the case, you need to take a very serious look at this "almost perfect" relationship and what it offers you. It is far from perfect if he is not concerned about you—both in and out of the bedroom.*

17. **My partner and I have a great relationship: good communication, good sex, and a lot of trust. But still, there is something I'm having a lot of trouble talking to him about and don't know the best way to raise the subject. I almost never have an orgasm during intercourse, so he is usually finished when I am still really aroused. How can I tell him that I would like him to masturbate me or stimulate me orally so that I can have my turn too? I don't want to insult him, but it often seems like he's more interested in his own pleasure than mine. Female, Senior**

*You say you have a really good relationship with your partner, so you should be able to talk about something as basic as him helping you to be sexually satisfied. If your* relationship is as good as you say it is, then what you are requesting is not something that he will see as a burden; on the contrary, it should make him very happy to hear you say what would please you. Having the conversation outside the bedroom will be important. Tell him you'd like to try these things, and he should be happy to oblige. If he is not interested in hearing about your ideas/needs, then I would examine relationship and decide if it is really heading in the right direction.

18. **What can a man do to last longer? Instead of him being a "one-minute wonder!" Female, First-Year**

First, I'd like to know who came up with that name—it sounds like an oxymoron. In many people's mind, he's no "wonder." It sounds like you're referring to someone who experiences premature ejaculation, where a man comes way too quickly. It's one of the most common sex problems for men and the easiest to fix. One common method used to help the man gain control (last longer) is to try the stop-start technique (developed by Dr. Semans in the 1950s—yes, that really was his name). Here, the partner stimulates the man's penis almost to the point of ejaculation, but then pauses until the urge to climax has passed. The process is repeated many times, each successive episode generally prolonging the amount of time between pauses. The man eventually develops the capacity to control his ejaculatory reflex in the presence of intense, prolonged stimulation. Another was developed by the famous sex therapists Masters and Johnson in the 1970s. Called the squeeze technique, it involves the man's partner **gently** squeezing his erect penis at the head or the base. The partner performs the "squeeze" as soon as the man indicates an urge to ejaculate and until the urge has passed (usually just a few seconds). Sex resumes and the process is repeated (usually three to four times) until the man learns ejaculatory control.

19. **Is it normal for a man, on occasion, not to be able to get an erection while being stimulated? Female, Sophomore**

Yes. Physical and emotional factors may interfere. For example, alcohol and other drugs can interfere with a man's *ability to get an erection. Also, a man who is overtired or overstressed is not at his best in anything. Be understanding and patient.*

**20. All the books say breasts are an erogenous part of the body. When my boyfriend touches mine, I don't feel a thing. Is there something wrong? Female, Junior**
*Each of us is unique and human diversity is wonderful. Some men want to touch a woman's breasts and will initiate lovemaking in that way. This may or may not be pleasurable to the woman, as the woman may find her turn-ons are elsewhere. You need to know where touch is most arousing to you and communicate to your partner where you would like to be touched and which way— so you both have the opportunity to be sexually excited together.*

**21. I know that a few beers can be a little relaxing before sex, but it seems like my girlfriend is to the point of being drunk when we have intercourse. Why? She says she likes it better when she's been drinking. Does it mean she's uncomfortable with me? Male, First-Year**
*It's more likely she's uncomfortable with herself. I don't know enough to guess why she's doing it, but it sure seems like something you two need to discuss. It must feel pretty strange to try to have an intimate relationship with your girlfriend when she's in such a state. It could be that she's really not comfortable with the sexual part of the relationship. Some people find it is easier to hide behind alcohol than to be honest about what's going on. If she is willing to talk with someone about her alcohol use, have her contact a local counseling center. If she is not, you may want to contact them yourself for some helpful suggestions on how to deal with this.*

**22. How does a woman *tactfully* tell her partner that she is not satisfied, that he needs to slow down and perhaps take time to do a few more things rather than just take care of himself—especially when he is convinced that he is doing everything well? How do you bring this up? Female, Senior**

*First of all, I would suggest the conversation take place outside the bedroom. You could begin by saying, "I think our lovemaking is nice, but I'd like to tell you a few things that would make it even better." Or you may want to ask him what pleases him sexually. Even if he responds that everything is fine, you could let him know that some things he does for you are fine but he must have some preferences also. Getting him to talk about what he really likes opens up the conversation for you to tell him what you like. It's important to be specific and let him know what turns you on, where, when, and so on. In bed, you may want to show him how you like to be touched. Keep in mind that no one likes to be criticized or made to feel stupid, so try to give your partner positive feedback. By communicating with each other, you will be better able to meet each other's needs.*

### 23. Is it true that "sex before the big game" weakens you? Male, Senior

*Most experts disagree with the athletic tradition of sexual abstinence before a big event. The prevailing advice is not to disturb your regular sex pattern. For instance, if you normally have sex two times a week, then continue to do so the week prior to your important event. This may help your athletic performance by keeping you relaxed. According to studies, relaxed athletes show greater aerobic capacity, less fatigue, and more speed than tense ones.*

### 24. Do men realize that women, in order to be satisfied sexually, need more than just a penis inside a vagina? Female, Junior

*Some men may not realize that the clitoris is strategically located outside and above the vaginal opening. For many women, stimulation around this area is essential for reaching orgasm. Such stimulation does not require intercourse or a penis. It's important for a woman to first find out for herself what feels good and then gently show her partner. He won't know unless someone tells him. Many men (and women) have been told that "real sex" means "penis-in-vagina" only; many of us recognize that sex involves much more than this.*

## 25. Does being an athlete really improve your sex life? Male, Sophomore

*To be a good lover, a man's most important physiological resource isn't a large sex organ but a strong heart. There are two reasons: (1) Erections depend on having a good supply of blood pumped from the heart. Unlike many sedentary people, athletes' arteries tend to be unclogged and healthy. (2) Long and vigorous lovemaking requires aerobic conditioning. This, too, poses no problems for athletes. Studies show that sex only raises your heart rate to about 60% of maximum. For most men, this intensity is high. For athletes, it's lower than the average workout. Perhaps the greatest connection between sex and athletics is the psychological one. As with any sport that's pursued regularly for fitness and enjoyment, athletics builds self-confidence and enhances self-image. When you look your best (and when other people tell you so), your sexuality is positively affected.*

## 26. Why do some people make so much noise during sex? If someone doesn't make a lot of noise, are they missing anything? Male, Junior

*First of all, it's important to have a bed that doesn't squeak. In terms of noise, well, some people are more open in their enthusiasm than others. Not everyone responds the same way to a surprise birthday party either.*

## 27. How often do most people do it? What's the average sex drive? I'm just wondering if I'm normal. Male, Junior

*Sex drive (or desire) varies greatly from person to person. Some people have sex twice a year, others have it twice a day. Your age, health, and how much schoolwork you have can all affect your desire. I would encourage you to think about what is comfortable for you and not look to some "national average" for assurance. In my own surveys of students enrolled in human sexuality, I'm always amazed at how many students assume everyone else is having so much more sex than they are. Do what feels comfortable for you and your partner.*

## 28. How much sex is too much sex? Male, Senior

*When it feels like it is too much for you and your partner. This is so individual, varying greatly from person to person.*

For example, there are some who would say sex more than once a month is too much, while others feel sex more than once a day is too much. In very extreme cases, sex may become like an addiction. If you feel sex is becoming almost compulsive or overwhelming—something you find yourself preoccupied with or obsessing about (as if it is the only reason for your being)—then it's time to seek out the assistance of a counselor.

**29. Why do guys seem so concerned about how they are in bed? My boyfriend seems too uptight—after sex he *always* asks how he did. I feel more like an Olympic judge than a sexual partner. Female, Junior**

*Men, more than women, are likely to suffer from performance fears. Male sexual role expectations can be devastating when the male is expected to orchestrate, initiate, determine, and be "ever ready" to perform sexually. Men are at an added disadvantage because they're less likely than women to admit their fear of perhaps not being sexually well above average. I suggest you slow down and talk with your partner about how you and he are feeling. It is important to deal with this issue now. Recognize that for some people, performance pressure can lead to "spectatoring." Just as we tend to be spectators at sports and other events, we sometimes become sexual spectators. We carefully watch, monitor, grade, and compare both our own sexual performance and that of our partner. It's almost as if we are withdrawing from our bodies and having our sexual experience as an observer. This can be destructive behavior because it takes so much away from the spontaneity of the experience and sets up certain standards of performance that we expect to meet or exceed each time we have sex. Spectatoring can produce anxiety and tension that greatly interferes with our sexual abilities.*

**30. Is there a documented number of sexual positions? Male, First-Year**

*There are exactly 529 possible positions for sexual intercourse, according to the Indian sexologist Yasodhara, commentator on Vatsyayana's* Kama Sutra. *Vatsyayana inflates the number considerably by including different arm and leg positions and sometimes other relatively inconsequential details.*

31. **Over the past few years I have had a few girlfriends and have always been careful and responsible about safe sex. My problem concerns something that happened to me last semester. One night after having too much to drink, I found I could not get an erection when I tried to have sex. I knew the reason was alcohol, but I can't seem to shake the fear that it will happen again whether or not I've been drinking. This worry just seems to always be there and actually gets worse on those occasions when having sex is likely to happen. How can I get rid of this worry and get on with my sex life? Male, Senior**

    *You've just described one of the most common sexual problems occurring among college students who go out drinking on any given night. In terms of your thinking process lately, I would ask you to consider ways to control your thoughts. Let's say you were with someone and becoming sexually aroused, but it wasn't the right moment. What would you do? You'd probably think of something else—something nonerotic—in order to calm yourself down. Well, the same technique can be used in reverse. If you start to worry about your performance, start thinking about something that will make you feel more aroused. Over time, your concerns should subside. You've made an important first step in recognizing the source of your problem, and you know it's mental, not physical. So now you just need to work on pushing those negative thoughts out of your head.*

32. **I heard once that vibrators cause some desensitization of the clitoris. Is this true? I use mine by applying it directly to my clitoris, so I need to know if it's bad for me in the long run. I wouldn't want to do something that would cause me to go without future pleasure. Female, Senior**

    *No need to worry. The vibrator is very safe and very effective in stimulating the clitoris. There is no evidence to suggest it will lead to any structural damage or desensitization—so enjoy! I assume that applying the vibrator directly on your clitoris leads you to orgasm most quickly. You might think about varying your technique (I know, you're probably thinking: why change a good thing?). What's great about the vibrator is that you can learn to extend and build to terrific orgasms. So you might want to vary your approach. For example, consider stimulating the clitoris for a few minutes and then "backing off" just before orgasm by stimulating the area around it, or putting a towel between the vibrator and the clitoris for a few minutes. By doing this several times, you may find your orgasm is much more intense, extended, and pleasurable. Enjoy!*

### 33. Does pot (marijuana) enhance sex? Male, Junior

*Some people report increased interest in sex under the influence of pot. It has been found to lead to relaxation and lowered inhibitions and therefore when used **in moderation** enhances sexual activity. Used in really high amounts, however, pot can have the opposite effect—leading to loss of desire for sex and inability to reach orgasm for some people. The only thing desired at this point is food.*

### 34. Why don't some people like oral sex? I tried to convince my girlfriend that it was normal stuff to do, but she isn't willing to even try. Male, Sophomore

*You bring up a good point: No one should ever be forced or coerced into any sexual behavior she or he is not comfortable with. In terms of who likes or does not like oral sex: depending on what study you look at, 10% to 30% of people surveyed found oral sex unusual, kinky, or very unappealing. Older adults report less experience with oral sex than younger people; those with more education are more likely to engage in oral sex than those with fewer years of schooling. There are many reasons why someone may feel uncomfortable with oral sex and wish to avoid it. Can you talk with your partner about what may be going on for her? One of the most obvious concerns relates to an individual's morals and attitudes about sex. Some believe that oral sex is simply wrong and conflicts with their personal code of acceptable behavior. Other reasons are unrelated to morality and concern the mechanics of the behavior itself. Women are often concerned that the man will ejaculate in her mouth and she will find that unpleasant. While it is not dangerous to swallow semen (assuming there are no infections), some women would rather not do so (since many students ask, semen is low in calories with only five calories in the average ejaculate). Both men and women worry that the smell or taste of the female genitals will be unpleasant or repulsive. In reality, female genitals that are washed with normal regularity have a natural fragrance that most people find attractive and enjoyable. If these are some of her concerns, perhaps they can be overcome by sensitivity, respect, and patience.*

# VII

**PASS WITH CARE**

## BIRTH CONTROL

There is no perfect method of birth control. The best method is the one that combines the greatest effectiveness with acceptance by the individual using it. If someone feels more comfortable and natural using a given method of birth control, he or she will be more inclined to use it correctly and consistently. An individual's attitude toward the chosen method makes all the difference; no method works if the individual doesn't use it.

Deciding on a method is a choice that should be based on several factors, including age, amount of sexual activity, lifestyle, medical history, and religious beliefs.

Most methods of birth control that we use today were not available in the past. We live in an era where it is sometimes taken for granted that people can control when and if they want children and how many. The advent of birth control has had a profound effect on women's roles. It has also affected the roles of men. Even though most methods of birth control directly involve the female's body, men are becoming increasingly aware of their responsibilities in contraception.

It's important to know that even though there are some medical risks with the Pill and some other birth control methods, these risks are minimal compared to the risks of pregnancy.

Some of the more common methods of contraception include:

## ORAL CONTRACEPTIVES ("THE PILL")

There are basically two types of birth control pills—the combination pill and the minipill. Combination pills contain estrogen and progestin and essentially fake a woman's body out to think she is pregnant, so no additional egg matures or is released. Minipills contain progestin, which thickens the cervical mucus to make it more difficult for sperm to pass through the cervix, and makes the lining of the uterus less receptive to a fertilized egg. Oral contraception is nearly 100% effective. A new kind of twist in birth control pills is the introduction of Seasonale, which allows you to take the pill for 3 months in a row without a period (versus 3 weeks in a row and then a 1 week break for a period); you have one period each season of the year.

## NORPLANT

Norplant consists of tubes containing progestin that are surgically placed under the skin of the woman's upper arm. It provides continuous contraceptive protection for as long as 5 years. While no longer available, women who are using Norplant may continue to do so.

## DEPO-PROVERA

A synthetic compound, Depo-Provera is similar to progesterone and is injected into the woman's arm or buttock. It protects the woman from pregnancy for 3 months by preventing ovulation.

## THE PATCH

Instead of swallowing a combination birth control pill each day, the woman places what looks like a Band-Aid (containing the same thing found in the Pill) on her abdomen, buttocks, upper torso, or upper arm each week. The patch, or Ortho Evra, slowly releases estrogen and progestin into the bloodstream. Three patches (used over the course of 3 weeks) are followed by a patch-free week (when menstruation occurs).

## THE RING

NuvaRing is a clear, flexible ring that is inserted into the vagina and worn for 3 weeks. Like the patch, it slowly releases hormones and after 3 weeks is removed for the fourth week (menstruation).

## INTRAUTERINE DEVICES (IUDS)

The IUD is a small object that is inserted into the uterus by a medical provider. The device is thought to prevent pregnancy by irritating the lining of the uterus, causing inflammation and the production of antibodies that may be toxic to sperm or a fertilized egg and may prevent implantation of the fertilized egg.

## THE DIAPHRAGM

The diaphragm is a shallow rubber dome attached to a flexible, circular metal spring. It varies in size from 2 to 4 inches in diameter, so a medical provider must fit a woman for her correct size. The diaphragm is used with spermicidal cream or jelly and inserted into the vagina up to 2 hours before intercourse to cover the cervix. It must be left in place for 6 to 8 hours after intercourse to allow the spermicide to kill any sperm.

# THE CERVICAL CAP

A cervical cap is a thimble-shaped device made of rubber that fits tightly over the cervix and is held in place by suction. Spermicidal cream or jelly is used with it (like the diaphragm), and it prevents sperm from entering the uterus.

# SPERMICIDES

Spermicides are chemicals that kill sperm. Inserted into the vagina before intercourse, spermicides come in several forms, including cream or jelly (to be used with a diaphragm), and foam or suppository (to be used alone or with a condom). It also comes in the sponge. The active ingredient is nonoxynol-9. Please note: Spermicides may irritate some people's tissue and can therefore increase one's the risk of getting an infection.

# CONDOMS

The male condom is currently the only form of male contraception. It is a thin sheath, made of latex or polyurethane. The condom works by being rolled over and down the shaft of an erect penis before intercourse. When the man ejaculates the sperm are caught inside the condom. It offers some protection against sexually transmitted infections. The female condom resembles the male condom in that it fits in the woman's vagina to protect her from pregnancy and sexually transmitted infections. Inserted like a diaphragm into the vagina, the female condom is a large, lubricated, polyurethane version of the male condom.

# EMERGENCY CONTRACEPTION

Also called post-coital contraception, emergency contraception refers to pills that are used after sexual intercourse primarily in three situations: when a woman has unprotected sex, when a contraceptive method fails, and when a woman is raped. The pills prevent pregnancy by interrupting ovulation, fertilization of the egg, or transportation of the egg to the uterus. They also make the uterine lining unreceptive to implantation. Although mistakenly referred to as "morning-after" pills, which implies they must be taken by the next morning, emergency contraceptive pills can be taken immediately or up to 5 days after unprotected sex (although effectiveness increases the sooner you take them).

*A note about abstinence:* **Abstinence refers to not having intercourse and avoiding any skin contact between the penis and vulva area. Its effectiveness depends on constant motivation with *no* exceptions. This does not mean you can't be intimate. There are other things you can do with your partner. Abstinence should be used when no contraception is available, in the presence of a sexually transmitted infection, or for 2 to 3 weeks following an abortion. It is the only method that is 100% effective.**

## PREGNANCY TESTING

The most common sign of pregnancy is a missed menstrual period. Nausea, breast tenderness, frequent urination, and tiredness may also be signs of pregnancy. Since none of these signs always means pregnancy, and since the uncertainty and anxiety are distressing, the thing to do is to have a pregnancy test.

It is very important to be tested as soon as pregnancy is suspected, for if you don't want to continue the pregnancy, the sooner you find out the better. The same holds true if you do desire to continue the pregnancy so that good prenatal care may begin. Pregnancy tests are available through your local Family Planning or Planned Parenthood clinic and private doctors. At-home pregnancy test kits are also available in drugstores.

The urine pregnancy test is the most commonly used. It can be performed 2 to 3 days after a missed menstrual period. A blood pregnancy test may be done as early as 3 weeks but is more expensive. If you are pregnant, a pelvic examination can be done to reveal how far along you are; counseling services are available to explore your options and give you resource information. Important and life-changing decisions will have to be made, including whether to terminate or carry the pregnancy to term. If you decide to carry the pregnancy to term, you will need to decide whether to keep the baby or give it up for adoption.

# ABORTION

For many women the decision about abortion is a painfully difficult choice to make. Most women experience a powerful mixture of feelings when an unwanted pregnancy is confirmed. Feelings such as fear, anger, sadness, confusion, and ambivalence may be overwhelming. Since abortions are safest when done early in pregnancy, it is important that a decision is made as soon as possible. If a woman has mixed feelings about being pregnant, it may be helpful to talk about those feelings with someone who cares about her. For many women, it is important to involve the man. Counseling services are available through Family Planning and Planned Parenthood clinics to discuss what her choices are and sort out feelings. Each woman and each situation is different. It is a personal decision; she must decide what is best and right for her.

Abortion is a medical procedure to end a pregnancy. The pregnancy and the lining of the uterus are removed. The most common method of abortion is a vacuum suction performed in the first 3 months and is available through clinics such as Planned Parenthood and private doctors. Initially, the vulva is sprayed with an antiseptic and a speculum is inserted into the vagina. The cervix is held firmly by an instrument and a local anesthetic is injected into the cervix. In a minute or so the area becomes numb. The cervical opening is dilated with narrow rods of increasing sizes, until the opening is about the size of a pencil. A suction tube is inserted into the uterus and the suction turned on.

While the procedure is being done, the woman is awake and will feel moderate to severe cramps as the pregnancy tissue is removed. The procedure takes about 15 minutes, followed by a few hours of recovery. For 2 weeks after the procedure, a woman can expect to experience bleeding, similar to her menstrual period. A follow-up visit is scheduled for two weeks later.

*Mifepristone (also called RU-486),* a chemical alternative to surgical abortion, has been widely used in France and is now available in the United States. Administered in the early weeks of pregnancy, it involves two injections. The first injection blocks the normal action of progesterone, thus causing the fertilized egg to break away from the uterine lining. The second injection two days later induces menstruation, causing the uterus to contract and expel the egg with the lining.

Although there are possible complications including infection and incomplete abortion, an abortion is considered much safer than childbirth and no more risky than a tonsillectomy.

For many women, the end of an unwanted pregnancy is a tremendous relief, but others may at the same time experience a return of some of the mixed feelings they had in deciding to have the abortion. The negative or confused feelings experienced after an abortion tend to pass away with time; for some this may happen quickly, for others more slowly. What's important to realize is that positive, negative, and ambivalent feelings are all natural after an abortion. Many women find acceptance of these feelings is made easier when sharing them with caring, supportive people.

## FAQS

1. **I got my girlfriend pregnant. What do I do? Male, Sophomore**

   *Don't panic and don't run. This is a human life you have started together and you both need to sit down and seriously talk about what you want to do. Legally, she has the power of decision whether to carry through with the pregnancy or abort. But if you continue to be caring and supportive with her, chances are that your views will be included in the decision. Pregnancy counseling and referral to medical services are probably available at your student health center and many local agencies, including Family Planning and Planned Parenthood.*

2. **Can you get pregnant the first time you have sexual intercourse or even if you don't "go all the way"? Female, First-Year**

*YES! In order for conception to occur, a sperm and an egg need to be present. If these conditions are met, it does not matter to the sperm and egg if this is your first time or tenth time. Also, in terms of not "going all the way"— meaning the penis did not actually enter the vagina—there is some concern if he does not ejaculate away from the vulva. If sperm are ejaculated close to the vaginal opening, there is a risk of pregnancy as well.*

3.  **If you are on the Pill, when is the most dangerous time to have sex? When do you ovulate? Female, Sophomore**
    *The Pill prevents ovulation from occurring, therefore there is no "dangerous time" (in terms of pregnancy) to have sex. Each pill contains a combination of the synthetic forms of estrogen and progesterone hormones normally found in a woman's body. The additional dosage provided by the Pill makes a woman's hormone level steady, similar to when she is pregnant. Therefore, the Pill acts to "fake out" a woman's body into thinking it's pregnant. It prevents pregnancy by: (1) preventing maturation and release of an egg each month from the ovaries, (2) making the uterine lining unreceptive for an egg, and (3) causing the cervical mucus to thicken, making it harder for sperm to penetrate. Once prescribed, a woman takes a pill every day for 21 days and then none for 7 days. During this time, menstruation occurs. Some brands contain seven additional pills of another color (placebos) to be taken during this time to help keep track of the days. Pills are taken every day at the same time to keep the hormone level the same. The Pill is estimated to be 99% effective in preventing pregnancy and can be obtained through your student health center or local Family Planning agency.*

4.  **How soon after conception can a woman know if she is pregnant? Female, First-Year**
    *One of the most widely recognized signs of pregnancy is a missed period. But it is important to remember that a missed or delayed period can be caused by a number of factors, including stress, emotional problems, hormonal disorders, or even worrying if you're pregnant. A urine test, available from your local health center or drugstore, can be done 2½ weeks after a missed menstrual period.*

5. **Can I get a woman pregnant if we have sex during her period? Male, Sophomore**

*Yes, if she happens to be ovulating near that time, as some women do. However, most women ovulate (release an egg) in the middle of their cycle—not during menstruation. For example, if a woman begins menstruation every 28 days, she typically ovulates on or around the 14th day after the start of her period. Unless you are willing to risk pregnancy, I suggest the two of you talk about an appropriate method of birth control. It's better to be safe than sorry.*

6. **Is there any time of the month when it is safe to have sex without a condom? Male, Senior**

*No, there isn't any really safe time. You're safest in a monogamous relationship, I suppose, if you can guarantee you and your partner are free of sexually transmitted infections (STIs) and not participating in another relationship where STIs might be brought into your relationship. In terms of pregnancy, there are times when it is safer and not safer. You are risking pregnancy if you don't use a condom, since ovulation (the fertile time) can vary from woman to woman.*

7. **Is it unhealthy to use birth control pills for several years? Female, Junior**

*It is considered safe to take the Pill for many years (up to the age of 35). In fact, the risks associated with pregnancy far outweigh the risks of being on the Pill. Experience shows that stopping and starting the Pill creates undesirable physical stress and increases the risk of pregnancy and menstrual irregularity. Do not stop the Pill until you have obtained and learned how to use another form of contraception. You should know that there are no routine medical benefits to stopping the Pill periodically or after a certain number of years. Please consult with your clinician before assuming it is necessary.*

8. **About six months ago my girlfriend and I decided to use the Pill as our form of birth control. After the start of its use, however, we both noticed a dramatic**

**decrease in her libido. Are there any alternatives to the Pill that don't have this side effect? If not, what can be done? Male, First-Year**

*There are certainly alternative forms of birth control available to you that would not necessarily affect one's sex drive or libido, including the IUD, diaphragm, and foam with condoms. However, if you would like to continue using the Pill, I would suggest your partner see her clinician to have her Pill adjusted. There are many types of birth control pills—each containing various levels of synthetic estrogen and progesterone. While the Pill is generally considered safe, it can cause side effects such as nausea, weight gain, and diminished sex drive. You should know that many researchers believe that loss of libido experienced by a small percentage of women using birth control pills is unrelated to the specific type and amount of estrogen or progestin that they contain. Others, however, believe that estrogen-dominant pills are less likely than progestin-dominant pills to decrease libido. If your girlfriend's sex drive has been negatively affected by using a progestin-dominant pill, switching to one with a greater amount of estrogen may be helpful.*

9. **I have a rather embarrassing problem. When I am with my girlfriend we have no problems until I put on a condom—then I lose my erection. I think it's the tightness that causes this, but I'm quite sure I'm not particularly large. I try not to make a big deal out of it, and I am very lucky to have such an understanding and loving girlfriend, but it's still very frustrating. I was wondering if this is a common problem, and what, if anything, I can do about it. Thank you. Male, First-Year**

*Your situation is not uncommon. Please remember that condoms come in different sizes. If tightness is a problem, how about switching to a larger brand. That should provide some relief. Many men—tight-fitting condom or not—experience some loss of sensation. Condoms take some getting used to. Rather than putting the condom on within seconds before intercourse, you may want to expand your sex play to include putting on the condom a few minutes before intercourse—so that you or your girlfriend can stimulate you to the point of another erection (think how much fun she'll have bringing it back up!). I might also suggest switching methods; for example, you might want to try using the female condom. It might be a nice alternative, providing protection from disease and pregnancy. You would not wear the condom—she would "wear" it. You may want to talk to someone about other alternative methods of protection.*

10. **Emergency contraceptive pills—where do we go to get it? We had sex without any birth control and we're worried she will get pregnant. I know we were stupid. . . . She's going on the Pill as soon as we get past this. Help! Male, Junior**

*Emergency contraception (also called "morning-after birth control" or "after-sex birth control") prevents a pregnancy from occurring only if used within 5 days of unprotected intercourse (although effectiveness is greater if taken within 72 hours/3 days). It reduces your chance of becoming pregnant by almost 90%. Approved by the FDA, it is available by prescription through your medical provider, Family Planning, Planned Parenthood, and other health clinics. It is sold under the name Plan B, and involves taking two pills containing progestin as soon as possible after unprotected sexual intercourse. The directions suggest taking one pill as soon as you can and the other 12 hours later. New research indicates that both doses can be taken at the same time. Be sure to follow up with the clinic about using an effective method of birth control. Please note: It is not an "abortion pill"—since you are not pregnant. Unfortunately, there has been some confusion around emergency contraception and RU-486, which is the drug now available to terminate a pregnancy within the first 2 months. RU-486 leads to abortion and you would see a medical provider for this once you know you are pregnant, unlike emergency contraception that you take to prevent the pregnancy from occurring. For more information on emergency contraception or for information on the closest provider, check out* **www.not-2-late.com**.

11. **Are there any types of birth control for men, other than things like condoms and sterilization? Male, Senior**

*Condoms and vasectomies appear to be the only options available for men—although some methods currently being researched appear to hold some promise. Currently, there are trials being conducted on a hormone injection (GnRH) that would block the development of sperm. The problem is that it seems to require daily injections—something most men won't find appealing. Another problem is that this hormone suppresses sexual desire, so it needs to be combined with another drug to offset this effect. Clinical trials involving weekly injections of a synthetic form of testosterone have also been found to reduce sperm production and may prove to be a promising new contraceptive for men. Another chemical, gossypol, has been tested as a nasal spray and appears to interfere with sperm production. Techniques to block the vas deferens (the tube connecting sperm with semen) are also being tested, including the use of injectable plastic liquid or temporary clips. It should be interesting to see what options are available to men in the next few years.*

12. **How many hours can go by before you remember to take a missed birth control pill but that you will still be protected from getting pregnant? Female, Sophomore**
    *You should talk with your health care provider. The usual suggestion is to take the Pill as soon as you remember; you may need to use a "backup" (e.g., condoms) for the rest of the month.*

13. **What are the chances of getting pregnant if you engage in unprotected sex during your period and you're on the Pill? Female, Senior**
    *The Pill is considered very effective in preventing pregnancy: 99%! A woman takes a pill (containing synthetic hormones) every day for 21 days, and then none (or placebos) for 7 days. During the 21 days, the Pill makes the body think it's pregnant—therefore, no egg is developed or released/ovulated. During the following 7 days of no pills (or while taking the placebos) a woman has her period. Theoretically, a women should not be at risk of pregnancy during this time—or at any time while on the Pill—since no egg has ever developed or been released. Sex is, therefore, not considered unprotected.*

## 14. How safe is the "pull and pray" method of birth control? Male, Junior

*I guess it depends on how strong your faith is—that is, if your prayer gets answered. Speaking of which, the Bible contains many references to contraceptive techniques, including coitus interruptus, or withdrawal ("pull and pray"). The story of Onan (Genesis 38:8–9), for example, implies knowledge of the withdrawal method. This method means that the man removes his penis from the vagina before ejaculating. Withdrawal has a first-year failure rate among typical users of about 20 to 25%. The reason is that the man may not withdraw in time. Because of its unreliability and high failure rate, withdrawal is considered an ineffective method of contraception. And one has to wonder, with all the effective methods available today, why someone would resort to using such a risky method to prevent pregnancy.*

## 15. I've heard that there is only one week a month you can actually get pregnant. Is this true? If so, when is this week? I always use condoms, but I want to know when during the month I can relax a little, because my biggest fear is getting pregnant at this point in my life. Female, Senior

*You sound like a great candidate for learning natural family planning—which is considered a method of birth control, but is actually a way to learn how your menstrual cycle works. Most women ovulate (release an egg) in the middle of their cycle. For example, if a woman begins menstruation every 28 days, she typically ovulates on or around the 14th day after the start of her period. The egg lives only 4 to 24 hours after ovulation. Sperm are most active within 48 hours after ejaculation. So, one way to avoid pregnancy is to avoid having intercourse around the time you ovulate. With natural family planning, you learn to recognize when ovulation occurs by taking your basal body temperature every day and charting it for months. Body temperature dips slightly just prior to ovulation, rises about 0.4 to 0.8 of a degree following ovulation, and remains high for the rest of the cycle. I suggest you get a book about this method or attend an evening class to learn more. Combining it with condom use will give you more peace of mind.*

### 16. Is condom breakage a common problem? If it does happen, what do you do to prevent pregnancy? Male, Senior

*An estimated 2 to 5% of condoms tear during use. Most of those failures are thought to stem from misuse, not inherent product flaws. The FDA, which regulates condoms as a medical device, reviews production records and examines stock at random. Should leaks turn up on 4 per 1,000 condoms in a run, the entire lot is thrown out. If you have the unfortunate experience of a condom breaking, you may want to consider having your partner insert an application of spermicidal foam immediately and then seeing someone at a local health center or Family Planning clinic in the next day or so. There you can discuss emergency contraception (after-sex birth control), which must be used within 72 hours (3 days) after unprotected intercourse. For future reference when purchasing condoms, check out* Consumer Reports *for their ratings of condoms.*

### 17. How long after I start the Pill do I have to wait to have unprotected sex (without fear of getting pregnant)? Female, Sophomore

*Most pills offer protection after the first week or so. It varies by pill type. Be sure to check with the health care provider who prescribed them.*

### 18. My boyfriend said that he read somewhere that going to the bathroom after sex will help to prevent pregnancy because it lets all the sperm out. Luckily I don't rely fully on this theory and I do use birth control, but I was just wondering if this had any truth behind it. Female, Junior

*No. I think the idea behind going to the bathroom after intercourse has gotten a bit twisted around. Those who work in the sexually transmitted disease clinics suggest you urinate after sexual intercourse to prevent bacteria from moving up the urethra. Therefore, urinating would have no effect on sperm that have been deposited into the vagina. In fact, by the time you step out of bed to run to the toilet, many of those sperm have already passed through the cervix into the uterus in search of an egg. I am happy to know you are using birth control for pregnancy prevention.*

## 19. When are we going to have more birth control options? It's the Pill, diaphragm, or condoms. I'm sick of waiting for something new! Female, Junior

*Well, you may have to wait a bit longer. Most of the new research focuses on extensions or improvements to the methods we currently have available. For example, some of the birth control devices under consideration include machines to determine when ovulation occurs. Some researchers have suggested that since ovulation is associated with an increase in water in the vagina, a tampon can be used to predict ovulation by measuring the amount of water it absorbs in a specified period of time. Others are looking for a substance in women's urine, blood, cervical mucus, or saliva that indicates ovulation is approaching. In terms of new spermicides, several experimental methods are being designed to create a barrier between the sperm and the egg. One of these is a water-soluble penile cap, which releases spermicide during intercourse; another is a vaginal ring that is inserted around the cervix and releases spermicide—it can remain in place for days. Some researchers are working on topical hormones that can be administered through nasal spray, and vaginal suppositories that contain progestin. Of course, we've all heard that there is supposed to be a male pill available fairly soon.*

*In terms of improving existing methods: There's the one-size-fits-all diaphragm that could be available soon in your local grocery store without a prescription, and there is an improved version of Norplant expected soon. Longer-lasting IUDs that provide 7 to 10 years of protection are currently available in Europe and there are now trials underway in the United States. Finally, one method reappearing on the market is the Today Sponge. In March 1999, Allendale Pharmaceuticals purchased the rights to manufacture and market the Today Sponge, which was the most popular over-the-counter contraceptive for women before it was taken off the market in 1995. It had been pulled from the market after the original manufacturer refused to add a water purification system that the FDA required. There was never any problem with Today Sponge's safety, just with the factory, according to the FDA.*

# VIII

DANGER:
PROCEED
WITH
CAUTION

### WHAT ARE STIs?

In the past, the expression *venereal disease* referred only to gonorrhea and syphilis. Today, however, a broader term, *STI,* or *sexually transmitted infection,* includes an extensive group of communicable diseases. The feelings of guilt and shame commonly associated with these infections are not helpful. After all, communicable diseases such as polio or tuberculosis, not usually thought of as sexually transmitted, may also be easily spread during sexual contact.

### WHO GETS STIs?

Well, first of all, plenty of people get STIs. *Each year, there are more reported cases of sexually transmitted infections than the common cold.* Basically, anyone having body contact with someone who is already carrying an STI can get one. An estimated 10 to 15 million Americans contract some STI every year. As a group, STIs are the most commonly reported communicable infections in the nation. The statistics on STIs are probably understated for two reasons: (1) Many people don't show symptoms of an infection and go undetected, and (2) many don't seek treatment due to embarrassment and/or fear. But even though the statistics available are limited, they are still alarming because they are evidence of an epidemic no one wants to acknowledge.

## WHY IS THERE AN STI EPIDEMIC?

There are several reasons for the epidemic number of STIs, but mainly the following:

1. Greater sexual freedom and general mobility of the population.
2. Lack of necessary education in schools at a time when sexual activity among teens is increasing.
3. The condom—an effective prevention for STIs—is not used as often as it should be.
4. Sexual activity is starting at an earlier age, and more people of every age are seeking a variety of partners.
5. There is a definite lack of public awareness about the extent and seriousness of STIs.
6. The Pill, which is more widely used than ever, changes moisture and alkalinity of the vagina, making the area more susceptible to STIs.
7. Research funding for developing vaccines against STIs is scarce.
8. Evolution of antibiotic-resistant strains increases difficulty of treatment.

## COMMON STIS

**Chlamydia.** Symptoms of chlamydia are often vague or nonexistent, with no symptoms early on in 70% of cases. In males, there is often a burning sensation with urination and an abnormal discharge; females may exhibit a mild itching or burning and irritation during urination. It is easily treated with tetracycline or erythromycin. However, left untreated, it can cause serious damage to the reproductive tract, leading to infertility.

**Gonorrhea.**   Symptoms of gonorrhea usually appear within 2 to 10 days after contact. As many as 80% of women and 20% of men have no symptoms. Left untreated, the infection could spread to the reproductive tract, leading to infertility. If a woman does have symptoms, they include burning urination, vaginal discharge, fever, or abdominal discomfort. A man might have a white or yellow discharge from his penis and painful urination. Gonorrhea is typically treated with a large dose of penicillin.

*Note about Pelvic Inflammatory Disease (PID):* **PID is a general term for an infection that travels from the lower genital tract (vagina and cervix) to the fallopian tubes and pelvic cavity. Symptoms may include pain in the lower abdomen, fever, and chills. It is often the result of untreated chlamydia or gonorrhea, and can lead to infertility in women.**

**Genital Warts (human papilloma virus, HPV).**   Genital warts are caused by viruses that remain in the body forever. There are over 100 types. Symptoms usually appear 1 to 3 months after direct contact. In moist body areas, warts may appear as soft, pink or red, cauliflower-like single or multiple clusters. On dry skin they appear as small, hard, yellow-gray warts. They are painless yet highly contagious. Podyphylin— a dark red resin—is used to burn off warts, or cryotherapy— the freezing of growths—can be used. Surgical methods may be used if growths are extensive. A few types can lead to cancer of the cervix, so a woman who tests positive for HPV should have a Pap smear every 6 months.

**Genital Herpes.**   Note there are two types of herpes: simplex 1, which usually occurs above the waist, like cold sores or blisters, and simplex 2, which usually occurs below the waist in the genital area. Symptoms for herpes II include a cluster of tender, painful blisters that appear in the genital area following direct contact with an open sore through petting, intercourse, or anal or oral sex. In women, vaginal and cervical blisters may go unnoticed. Other symptoms include headaches, fever, possibly swollen glands, and painful urination due to open sores. The first outbreak is usually most severe, lasting up to 4 weeks. While the virus stays in the body for a lifetime, 25% of those infected never have recurrences.

The virus can be reactivated by stress, hormonal changes, sunbathing, food allergies, cold, or fatigue. Recurrences are less severe and of shorter duration, lasting 1 to 2 weeks. There is no cure. However, symptoms might be relieved by taking warm baths several times daily, washing the sores gently with a germicidal soap, drying them carefully, and dusting them with talcum powder. Avoid tight-fitting underwear and creams or ointments on sores. A medication called acyclovir (brand name Zovirax) may be prescribed. For women, risk of cervical cancer is increased with genital herpes; therefore, Pap smears are recommended every 6 months. For men, herpes has been linked to prostate, penile, and testicular cancer.

**Syphilis.** Symptoms of syphilis appear 10 to 90 days after direct contact with infectious sores or rash and proceed through a number of stages if left untreated. In the primary stage: chancre sores appear where bacteria entered the body and disappear in 1 to 5 weeks naturally, without treatment—though the disease is still present. In the secondary stage: within 6 to 8 weeks of chancre, a rash, flulike symptoms, mouth sores, patchy baldness, and swollen glands appear. These may last from a few months to up to 2 years. If left untreated, symptoms disappear and the disease progresses to the tertiary stage. The disease then attacks internal organs in a third of untreated cases, leading to possible brain damage, insanity, paralysis, heart disease, and death. Therefore, early detection is important. Treatment involves antibiotics.

**Hepatitis B (HBV).** Hepatitis is a virus that causes liver disease. Type A is usually contracted through the mouth from contaminated food or water, while Type B is transmitted sexually through semen and vaginal secretions. Symptoms include loss of appetite, nausea, diarrhea, yellowing of the skin, and enlargement of the liver. It can lead to destruction of the liver and other organs and death. There is no cure, although a vaccination is available.

**Nonspecific Urethritis (NSU).** Nonspecific urethritis, sometimes called nongonococcal urethritis (NGU), refers to any inflammation of the male urethra that is not caused by gonorrhea; chlamydia accounts for half of the cases of NSU. Symptoms usually appear within 1 to 3 weeks. Usual symptoms in men include a clear, thin, white discharge, frequently present only in the morning, and mild irritation when urinating. Antibiotics are frequently used to treat NSU.

**Vaginitis.** Certain common vaginal infections are now grouped with STIs because some of these conditions can be spread through intercourse. It is normal for all women to have some degree of vaginal discharge. It has a mild but inoffensive odor and is not irritating to the body. (Since the body has its own cleaning mechanisms, most feminine hygiene sprays and douches are unnecessary and can lead to irritation.) Vaginitis, however, is usually characterized by some unusual discharge and odor. Treatment often includes vaginal suppositories and/or antibiotics.

  A. *Candidiasis Yeast Infection.* This type of vaginitis is caused by the overgrowth of a fungus. Symptoms are brought on by body changes. The organism is frequently found in the mouth, vagina, and rectum without any symptoms. Increased incidence is also found in women taking the Pill. A thick, white, cream cheese–like vaginal discharge occurs with a yeastlike odor, itching, and irritation. Antifungal creams and suppositories used for treatment are sold over-the-counter (e.g., Monistat and Gyne-Lotrimin).
  B. *Trichomoniasis.* Trichomoniasis is caused by a one-cell parasite. Symptoms show in 1 to 4 weeks. During the infectious state, women have yellow-green or gray, thin, foamy vaginal discharge with a foul odor and irritation. It often flares up just prior to or during menstruation. Incidence increases for women on the Pill. Both the woman and her infected partner will be treated with metronidazole (Flagyl).
  C. *Bacterial Vaginosis.* Bacterial vaginosis or *gardnerella vaginalis* is caused by a bacteria. Symptoms in infectious state include creamy white or gray vaginal discharge and foul odor (sometimes described as fishy). It can lead to serious upper reproductive tract infection. The antibiotics of choice are metronidazole (Flagyl) or clindamycin. Sexual partners may also be treated to reduce the risk of reinfection.

Some overall practical advice on prevention and alleviation of vaginal infections include the following helpful hints: keep clean; avoid vaginal deodorants and deodorant tampons and pads; avoid wearing nylon underwear, tight pants, and pantyhose; use caution in douching; keep sugar and refined carbohydrate intake low; avoid intercourse for the duration of the infection; get plenty of rest and relaxation; and most importantly, communicate with your partner(s). When in doubt about infections, men should always use a condom.

**AIDS (Acquired Immune Deficiency Syndrome).**   This fatal disease, which was first identified in 1981, involves the destruction of the immune system, leaving a person susceptible to all viruses and bacteria. It is caused by the human immunodeficiency virus (HIV) that is transmitted through the exchange of bodily fluids (blood, semen, vaginal secretions), primarily in sexual activity and IV drug use. Upon infection with HIV, a person typically shows no sign of infection for many years. In the meantime, transmission of the virus to sexual partners is possible. A blood test for the HIV antibody is available. HIV attacks the body's immune system by destroying the T-cells, making the body vulnerable to opportunistic infections and cancers, especially pneumocystic pneumonia and Kaposi's sarcoma, which are the primary causes of death among most people with AIDS. There is no cure for AIDS as yet, but further study is being done. Following safer sex practices such as using a latex condom can control the spread of the virus.

**Parasites.**   Some forms of STIs are not really infections at all but are body infestations. The two most common are *pubic lice* (crabs) and *scabies*. Pubic lice and scabies are easily spread by close physical contact, especially intercourse, but also while dancing or just holding hands or cuddling. These "bugs" can be acquired from bedding, another person's clothes, and yes, even the dreaded toilet seat. Symptoms usually appear in 4 to 6 weeks, producing severe itching. Kwell lotion is usually prescribed for the treatment.

**Sex-Related Genital Infections.**   Some genital infections result from the spread of bacteria from a place where they do no harm (such as the rectum) to a place where they can cause much trouble (urethra, bladder, prostate gland).

A. *Cystitis.* This urinary tract infection is an infection of the bladder. Nearly every woman gets it sometime. Symptoms include an almost constant, strong (even painful) urgency to urinate frequently when there is nothing to come out, and a severe burning when the urine is passed. Strong color and blood during urination are also possible symptoms, and sufferers may have low back or abdominal pain or fever. The bacteria involved may have been pushed up to the bladder during vigorous or repeated intercourse. Cases of cystitis in men are rare because the urethra in men is longer and bacteria don't get a chance to get to the bladder. Treatment involves antibiotics.

B. *Prostatitis.* This infection is an inflammation of the prostate, which surrounds the male's urethra near the site of the bladder. Symptoms include tender prostate, fever, chills, and difficulty urinating. Usually it is caused by bacteria, which is more difficult to treat. Symptoms vary; some men feel pain in their lower back, and urination may be frequent, difficult, or burning. There may also be drips or discharge from the urethra. Treatment, usually with antibiotics, is difficult.

## SMART SEX

We have the knowledge we need to protect ourselves against unwanted pregnancy and disease. Why don't we use it? Why do people still risk pregnancy and disease by having unprotected intercourse?

One reason is the abundance of popular myths regarding sexuality—like "nice girls don't plan ahead," or "everything should be spontaneous." We need to turn these ideas around. It's **not** bad to be prepared—it's mature. **Anyone** who has sex without protection is inviting trouble.

Smart sex includes shared responsibility and candid talk that should take place before genital contact occurs. It is imperative to discuss birth control and the possibilities of having an STI. Without discussion we only have embarrassed silence and widespread ignorance about unwanted pregnancy and STIs that constitute serious health problems among young adults.

Remember: If you're mature enough to have sex, you're mature enough to use protection, and to use it correctly and consistently.

**Some guidelines for smart sex:**

1. *Condom use.* When put on and taken off properly, the condom is one of the best methods for preventing STIs.
2. *Limited partners.* Having sex with one person who is having sex with only you will greatly reduce the chances of being infected. The more partners you have, the greater the risk. Also, be more selective about your partners. One-night stands, pickups, and sexual intimacy with someone you hardly know pose a greater risk.
3. *Cleanliness.* Washing with soap and water before and immediately after intercourse may wash away some germs. However, these germs may penetrate skin before you get a chance to wash. Therefore, washing is only an aid.
4. *Urination.* Urinating immediately after contact can flush some germs out.
5. *Regular checkups.* If you are sexually active, have a regular annual checkup. If you have symptoms, go immediately to your medical provider or clinic.
6. *Simultaneous treatment.* Notify your sexual partner(s) that you are infected. Avoid intercourse and oral sex until both you and your partner(s) are fully treated.
7. *Observation and communication.* Before you have contact, **look** for any suspicious sores, rashes, or discharges and discuss them with your partner. Don't let the myth that sex has to be spontaneous to be romantic interfere with good sense. Remember: There is no such thing as a romantic STI.

**Note: In most cases, untreated STIs can lead to serious complications. Also, if you become pregnant, virtually every STI has the potential to affect the unborn fetus or newborn in some way.**

## FAQS

**1. I know it's important to ask your sexual partner to wear a condom, but how should I approach the issue? I'm not comfortable discussing it. Female, Sophomore**
*Anyone you know well enough to be sleeping with, you should know well enough to talk about protection with.*

*However, I recognize that talking about sex isn't easy. But in this age of "fatal sexuality"—where people can die from unprotected sexual intercourse—it is really important that you talk about using condoms. Before you end up in bed, talk with your partner about your need to have sex safely. If he's a former Boy Scout, he'll understand the concept of being prepared. If he's ever played sports, he'll understand how important it is to wear protective gear before you play the game.*

## 2. How can I stay protected from disease with a one-night stand without using a condom? I don't like using them. Male, First-Year

*I'm not sure you can. The use of latex condoms has been found to be an excellent protection from both pregnancy and disease. Someone once recommended that in order to get used to using a condom during sexual intercourse, you might try masturbating with two condoms—then when you have sex with one it feels like a breeze! A more common practice that some men say makes the condom more appealing is to put some lubrication on the head of the penis before rolling the condom on.*

## 3. Should I be concerned if my girlfriend has been diagnosed with vaginitis? Male, Sophomore

*Because the vagina provides a moist and convenient passage from a woman's abdominal organs to the outside world, it also makes women vulnerable to a variety of vaginal irritations and infections. The general term* vaginitis *covers them all, whether or not the irritation has anything to do with being sexually active. Sometimes a distinction is made between nonspecific vaginitis and cases of vaginitis that are due to known specific infections like chlamydia, trichomonas, gardnerella, yeast, and venereal warts. Should men be concerned about a sexual partner who has vaginitis? Yes, because the same organisms that infect the vagina can invade the male urethra during intercourse and spread to the prostate or other internal sexual organs. If a woman has vaginitis, her sexual partner should also be tested.*

### 4. Is it okay for a woman to swallow semen? Female, First-Year

*Only if you are sure he is not infected. If, however, he is infected with HIV (the virus causing AIDS), there is a risk that you could become infected as well.*

### 5. Is a test for syphilis automatically done during a gynecological exam? How is the test done? Female, Sophomore

*No, a blood test for syphilis must be requested. The initial sign of syphilis is a chancre (a round, ulcerlike lesion with a hard, raised edge, resembling a crater), which appears at the point where the bacteria entered the body. For men, the chancre typically appears on the penis or scrotum; for women, the chancre often appears on the vaginal walls, the cervix, or the vulva. It is painless and may not be noticed, disappearing after 1 to 5 weeks. Unless you have a pelvic exam during this time, syphilis may go unnoticed. Although the chancre disappears, the disease does not— it has now entered the bloodstream and, left untreated, will continue to attack the body, leading to serious consequences, including death. Therefore, a blood test is done to determine the presence of antibodies to the bacterium (T. pallidum) that causes syphilis. This test does not give accurate results until at least 4 to 6 weeks after the person has been infected. If you are concerned, please call your student health center or local STI clinic. Syphilis is easily treated with penicillin.*

### 6. How long can you be HIV-positive without showing any signs of AIDS? Does being HIV-positive always mean you will eventually develop AIDS? Male, Sophomore

*A person can become infected with HIV and not show any signs of infection for many years. An infected individual will test positive to an HIV antibody test, but will show no signs of being infected. That's one reason this disease is so scary—many people are infected and do not know it. Some studies suggest it is about 10 years before a person who is HIV-positive develops AIDS. With new drug treatments it is hoped that this can be prevented.*

7. **Is it the man's or the woman's responsibility to provide the condoms? Female, First-Year**
   *Both people in the relationship need to take responsibility for protecting each other from pregnancy and disease. If you are not ready to be responsible for protection, you are most likely not ready for sex. Communicating with your partner before you find yourself sexually involved will be essential to ensure you are both willing to use protection.*

8. **Do women really have to worry about HIV? I heard that women represent only a small fraction of cases of AIDS, so what's the big deal? Female, Junior**
   *Well, for starters, it is a big deal because HIV can kill you. There is no question that the predominant transmission of HIV in the United States is still male-to-male. And, while women represent a smaller percentage of HIV-infected individuals, that doesn't mean you shouldn't be concerned. Are you suggesting we should wait until women represent a higher percentage of HIV-positive people? I suggest we* **all** *pay attention and do what we know we should to protect ourselves from infection.*

9. **What are the symptoms of genital warts? Male, Senior**
   *Genital warts are determined by visible inspection. HPV (human papilloma virus) causes genital warts, which is a very common virus, infecting about 1 out of every 4 sexually active people. The warts typically appear on the genitals as soft, pink, painless single or multiple growths resembling a small cauliflower. In men, they may appear on the penis, foreskin, and scrotum, and within the urethra. In women, they may be found on the vulva, in the vagina, and on the cervix. The warts begin to appear 1 to 3 months after contact and are diagnosed visibly. They may be removed by freezing, burning, dehydration with an electrical needle, or surgery. Although such treatments may remove the warts, please be aware that they do not rid the body of the virus—so there may be recurrences.*

10. **What do you do when you find out that you have an STI and your partner won't get tested? Male, Junior**
    *This is a very serious situation. Have you tried to find out why your partner won't be tested? Is it fear? Shame? Denial? Is your partner afraid to know the test results? Are*

*there issues of who gave this disease to whom? Is there an issue of faithfulness? Maybe your partner has no symptoms—does she or he realize some people show no signs when infected? Why is your partner willing to risk being infected (and the potential damage to the reproductive organs) and also willing to risk passing it back to you if you continue to be sexually involved? If your partner won't be tested, how can you continue in a sexual relationship? Why is your partner willing to risk disease and possibly infecting other (you and future) partners? I can only imagine how this has impacted your relationship. While you cannot force your partner to be tested, you can decide if you want to continue to participate in this relationship. You need to think seriously about it and stand firm on your desire to take care of yourself.*

**11. Why isn't there more public awareness of HPV? We hear so much about HIV/AIDS, but HPV affects many more people and is potentially as lethal (cancer). Female, Senior**

*HIV/AIDS is indeed a very scary thing. But you're right, AIDS is only one of many STIs, although certainly the most deadly and frightening. Nearly every day you pick up the newspaper and read about AIDS, yet other STIs pose much wider threats. In a study of 16,000 students on 19 U.S. college campuses, HIV (the virus that causes AIDS) was found in 30 blood samples or 0.2% of the students in the sample. However, chlamydia trachomatous (the bacterium that causes chlamydia) and HPV (human papilloma virus, the organism that causes genital warts) were each found in 10% of the college population. Chlamydia, virtually unheard of a generation ago, is now the most common bacterial STI in the United States. It's as common as the common cold (think about how many people you know right now with colds!).*

*The same study found that college students were pretty knowledgeable about AIDS. However, many were unaware that chlamydia can go undetected for years and, if left untreated, can cause pelvic infections and infertility. Most students were completely ignorant of HPV, which is linked to cervical cancer. Yet the Centers for Disease Control estimate that as many as 1 million new cases of HPV infection occur each year in the United States—more than syphilis, genital herpes, and AIDS combined. Whereas 1 to 1.5 million Americans are thought to be infected with HIV, about 56 million are infected with other STI-causing viruses. So, you're right. AIDS is a problem. However, we need not forget about the other sexually transmitted infections. We need to be educated on all of them.*

## 12. Can you get genital herpes from someone with a cold sore giving you oral sex? Female, Senior

*Yes. Genital herpes infection is caused by exposure to the herpes simplex virus type 1 (HSV 1) or herpes simplex virus type 2 (HSV 2) through sexual contact. The two viruses are not different clinically, as both cause the same painful symptoms. HSV 1 initially was associated with oral infection (cold sores and fever blisters around the mouth) and HSV 2 with genital infection (blisters on the penis or vulva). Over the past 30 years, however, the increased popularity of oral sex has led to an almost equal probability of transferring either form from mouth to genitals and vice versa. A person with herpes can also transfer it to other parts of his or her own body, including the eyes, by touch (autoinoculation). A 2- to 12-day incubation period follows transmission of the virus. There is no cure, but there is treatment to speed the healing of the painful blisters. An estimated 20 to 30 million people are presently infected with genital herpes in the United States. You should know that the virus can be easily spread by even a quick, casual kiss, and thus it should not be assumed that a person with oral herpes got it from performing oral sex. By the way, not all mouth ulcers are caused by the herpes virus; they can also be caused by bacteria, allergic reactions, or autoimmune (canker sores) responses. However, fever blisters and most cold sores are herpes.*

# IX

```
┌─────────────────────┐
│ ┌─────────────────┐ │
│ │                 │ │
│ │     TRAFFIC     │ │
│ │                 │ │
│ │     CIRCLE      │ │
│ │                 │ │
│ │     AHEAD       │ │
│ │                 │ │
│ └─────────────────┘ │
└─────────────────────┘
```

## GENDER/SEX ROLES

Traditionally, men and women have been raised to be oppo-
sites, to be half people. Rigid gender/sex role conditioning
has discouraged the development of the full range of our potential and limits our sexuality. Conditioning has shaped men
to be aggressive and dominant, and encouraged women to be
passive and subordinate. In sexual behavior, these separate
roles have created a double standard. Men have been taught
to be "on the make" and interested in "scoring" as many
women as possible. Women have been taught to be "attractive"
while concealing their sexual desires, to be nonsexual. This
double standard, or difference in roles, where women are supposed to resist and men are supposed to conquer, has greatly
interfered with many couples' sexual enjoyment. These different roles may frustrate intimate relationships because they
are filled with assumptions and misunderstandings.

Liberating ourselves from these preconceived roles can lead
us to more responsible, caring, and enjoyable relationships.

Freed from the "shoulds" of male and female roles, people are able to discover themselves in a more realistic manner. Today men and women are beginning to acknowledge their full range of feelings, including sexual desires and tenderness toward others. Becoming aware of our total selves, not just half, allows us to create more satisfying relationships. Viewing each other as human beings first, and by gender second, gives us the freedom to be more fully human.

## SEXUAL ORIENTATION

The word *homosexuality* looks just like all the other entries in the dictionary, just as homosexuals appear to be like other people in society. The analogy serves to put homosexuality in a perspective for the heterosexual person. A homosexual cannot be defined as psychologically disturbed, effeminate (for men), butch (for women), or as a threat to heterosexual society. Homosexuals are in every walk of life and are your brothers and sisters, teachers, and friends.

Homosexuality is the condition of being sexually attracted to members of one's own sex. The only basis for deciding whether or not one is homosexual is a continuing erotic preference for partners of the same sex. Many gays are forced to live "in the closet," in constant fear of discovery. Homosexuals have been banned from military service, ministry, and teaching, and have been denied housing, jobs, and bank loans. There are also successful and recognized members of society who are gay and some who are "out of the closet." People are individuals and live the way they want to; sexual orientation should not determine anyone's lifestyle.

Although some research has been done on the subject, it is not yet known exactly why someone is homosexual, bisexual, or heterosexual. It is presumed, though, that sexual orientation is determined by the age of 5, and possibly before birth. We do know, however, that one or a few homosexual experiences do not make a person homosexual. Homosexuality/heterosexuality is a continuum, not an either/or situation.

Authorities have estimated that perhaps 1 out of every 10 to 15 people is gay. Therefore, the number of gays would total many millions. Homosexual lifestyles, tastes, and personalities vary as widely as do heterosexual ones. It's important to remember that there is more to a person than his or her sexual orientation. Homosexuals, just like heterosexuals, are people first.

## GENDER IDENTITY

*"It's a boy!" "It's a girl!"* When we are born, such proclamations are based on our anatomical appearance. A baby born with a penis is said to be a boy, while a baby born with a vagina is said to be a girl. For most people, this is fine—since there is a feeling of consistency between their anatomical sex and their assigned gender. However, for some people, there is an inconsistency between their assigned gender and the gender they actually feel themselves to be. It's important to recognize that while sex is rooted in biology (what's between our legs), gender is rooted in our culture and how we think of ourselves (what's between our ears). There can be great variation in how a person identifies him- or herself. If there is inconsistency between one's sex and gender, it may be called a gender identity disorder, gender dysphoria, or more commonly transgender.

*Transgender* is an umbrella term for those people whose gender identity differs from the sex they were assigned at birth. The term may include but is not limited to transsexuals, intersex people, cross-dressers, and other gender-variant people. In the case of *transsexuals*, this term typically refers to people who feel they are trapped in the body of the "wrong sex." These people feel they are not really the gender of their genitals. Their personalities don't fit their anatomical sex and they may desire to undergo sexual reassignment procedures that involve hormonal and surgical interventions to correct the inconsistency.

*Transsexual* should not be confused with *transvestite* (see the word *vest* in the name and think of someone who wears clothing of the other gender, or cross-dresses). Men and women cross dress for many reasons, for example, as a way to challenge gender roles, as a form of gender relaxation, or as a way to get in touch with one's masculine or feminine side. Others, such as drag queens, cross dress as a sexual or political statement. Still others—those known as transvestites—wear clothes of the other sex for the purpose of sexual arousal. As you can see, "It's a boy!" or "It's a girl!" is not always so easy to define. A number of organizations are available to assist those with gender identity concerns.

## FAQS

### ABOUT WOMEN:

1. **Why do women always want serious commitments? I've never been able to have just a casual dating relationship with anyone I've ever dated. Male, Junior**

   *I think it's true, generally, that many (not all) women prefer commitment to casual dating relationships. If what you want is a casual friendship without a commitment, it is important to be clear about this both with yourself and with the women you meet and date. Sometimes men implicitly make promises about "always being there" for the other person without realizing it. Some examples of implicit promises include statements such as, "You're really special," "I've never met anyone like you before," or "I can't wait to see you again." Think through your initial relationships of the past and see if you have made such promises, either verbally or nonverbally, in order to enhance your relationship at the time.*

2. **Why do girls say they want to have relationships with nice guys but go out with jerks (and keep going back to them when they treat them like dirt)? Male, Sophomore**

   *Often, our past experience—even as children—preconditions us to feel more comfortable, more at home, in destructive relationships. People who have grown up with damaging experiences often can change the direction of their lives with the help of counseling. Of course, not every woman seeks this type of relationship; but for those who do, counseling and psychotherapy are often helpful.*

3. **Why do women go to the bathroom in pairs or groups? Male, Sophomore**

   *There are probably many reasons: safety in numbers, someone to hold the door, so they can have someone to talk to. Research has shown that in a heterosexual setting, where there are two to three couples, men tend to dominate the conversation. In addition, should one of the two women get up to use the restroom, the one who stays behind is often left out of the conversation. Going to the bathroom together allows women a space in which to talk with each other.*

4. **Why do girls play "head games"? Why can't they just be honest about who they are and what they feel? Male, Senior**

   *Not everyone does this. However, to understand why some people (males and females) might do this, realize: We all want to be liked. In new relationships, we tend to present an idealized version of ourselves. We want to put our "best foot forward," hoping the other person will like us. I'm not sure what you mean by "head games," but my guess is that behind the facade is a person not yet ready to risk her true self. Be supportive and patient, and when it is safe, your friend may be more open with you.*

5. **Why do women say they want a guy who's sensitive, and then when they find one, it's not good enough and they want a "macho man"? Male, Junior**

   *It sounds as if you've been in a relationship where this has happened. Many women look for a combination or balance in traits and want both sensitivity and strength at appropriate times. Sensitivity, gentleness, and warmth are wonderful traits in a man, and many women certainly seek these traits in their friends and lovers. Many women also look for strength, which may or may not be "macho." If your relationship did not work out, there are surely others who will be interested in your particular mix of characteristics.*

6. **Why do women feel that after sex you must cuddle? Male, Junior**

   *Not surprising, a woman asked: "Why do men roll over or get up/leave immediately after sex?" Much of it has to do*

*with what sex means to us. If sex means simply thrusting
a penis into a vagina until he comes, then that person may
feel that what has been desired has been accomplished.
Another may see sex more broadly—as an expression of
connection (both physical and emotional). Therefore, that
person may not see the man's orgasm as a sign that sex
is over. Talking with your partner beforehand about your
views on sex is important. Hopefully, with more understanding, there will be less resentment later.*

### 7. How do you know if a girl is experienced? Male, First-Year

*By "experienced" I assume you mean sexually experi-
enced. Well, it's not as if you can look at someone and "tell"
what's happened to her sexually, if that's what you're asking. If it's really that important to you, why don't you just
ask her.*

### 8. Why do women always seem to get so upset that men fall asleep after sex? Male, Sophomore

*One reason might be because she is wide awake. This
tends to be a problem in relationships where "after sex"
means after he has had his orgasm and sex ends—without
her having reached orgasm, too. She's still aroused and he,
feeling satisfied, is now tired. After orgasm, both men **and**
women feel tired, so you may want to consider this. It's as
if a chemical change has taken place and we feel the need
to rest/sleep. Another reason for her being upset may be in
the way she views sex versus how he views sex. Many
studies have suggested that women tend to see "sex" as
something that includes what happens before (like talking,
kissing, and touching) and what happens after orgasm
(more talking, kissing, and snuggling). So when he falls
asleep after ejaculation, thinking the interaction is over, she
may be feeling like the interaction is only half over.*

### 9. Why do women have a harder time watching porn movies than men? Male, Senior

*I'm not sure this is true for all women. Women interpret
pornography in different ways. Some find it sexist, some
find it a form of fantasy, like dreams and the movies
we run in our heads when we masturbate or have sex.
However, for those women who don't enjoy watching a*

*porn movie, I would guess it may be because these videos are typically made by men for men's enjoyment. Plus, old notions still linger, such as "good girls aren't supposed to enjoy sex." You may be surprised to know that half of the adult videos in the United States are bought or rented by women alone or women in couples.*

## ABOUT MEN:

1. **Are guys always ready for sex? And why do most guys stop after they are satisfied? Female, First-Year**

   *In response to your first question: It's hard to generalize; some men are always ready and some men aren't. There are women who like sex as much as men, and some women who like it more than men. In response to your second question: Some men stop after they are "satisfied" because that's what they have learned. The message has been that sex ends with **his** orgasm. If you are experiencing this in your own relationship and it is a problem for you, you need to communicate this to your partner. He may not realize that his self-centered behavior bothers you. There are other ways of experiencing sexual enjoyment together where you can both feel satisfied.*

2. **Why do men use women for sex and how can a woman tell, before she sleeps with a guy, if he is just using her for sex? Female, Sophomore**

   *Not all men use women in this way. Many guys want to have sex only within the parameters of a meaningful relationship. A meaningful relationship is not an instant achievement; one doesn't develop a meaningful relationship at a single party, in a casual conversation, or because you bumped into each other in a bar. Friendships take a while to build, and develop best on a basis of shared interests and experiences. If there is no meaningful relationship and no friendship, there may be no way for you to tell why another person wants to share a sexual relationship with you.*

3. **Why are men "studs" if they have sex a lot, but women are "sluts" if they do? I mean, why is it that guys never**

**think of themselves as sluts, but they are always ready to point the finger at women? Doesn't it take two to tango? Female, Senior**

*Someone once said women have only three roles: prude, tease, or slut. Unfortunately, the double standard is alive and well. It's fading—but not fast enough. You're right: It's not valid. You're dealing with generations of cultural values and this one has been very slow to change.*

4. **Do men really enjoy oral sex, or do they do it just to please their partner? Female, Junior**

   *Some men (and some women) enjoy oral sex and some do not. That's a decision for you and your partner to talk about. Why don't you ask him?*

5. **Why is it that men have a harder time being close? Why isn't intimacy as important to them as it is to women? Female, Senior**

   *Many men do not get the opportunity to build "intimacy skills" while growing up. Women tend to have more practice in this area. Little girls are allowed to stay close and connected to their mothers, while boys are "pushed out of the nest" so to speak. Girls are allowed to touch each other—while men can touch only in specific situations (for example, during sports or during sex). Research has indicated that women are more likely to call a friend "just to catch up," while men talk to each other about doing things. It's more acceptable for women to share feelings; many men are still being raised to think it's "unmanly" to cry or say they feel hurt. It takes time to unlearn some of these messages and to recognize the benefit of feeling free to express yourself and feel close to someone. Developing intimacy takes time. Fortunately, more and more men are recognizing their desire to develop this ability.*

6. **Men claim they are looking for independent women. Yet when they get involved with one, they often can't handle it and run away. Why? Female, Sophomore**

   *This is complicated. Some men may be genuinely interested in a relationship with an independent woman, while others may say they are and realize later that they really are not. Keep in mind: We don't always look for what we really want, and we don't always say what we really want; our desires may be elsewhere. It may be popular or politically correct to say you want an independent woman. In addition, we don't always consciously know what we really want.*

**7. Is it true that women only have sex for love and men only have sex for pleasure? Female, Junior**

*In other words, you seem to be suggesting that women look for a reason; men look for a place. I certainly hope you understand that while there are differences in the way some women and some men approach sex, we're not so easy to categorize. It's just as reasonable to say some women look for pleasure and some men look for love. I suspect most people look for a combination of both. This issue would make for an interesting late-night discussion among friends.*

## SEXUAL ASSAULT

Rape is an act of violence and aggression. It's a life-threatening invasion of a person's body, with the goal of the assailant being physical and sexual control of the victim rather than sexual gratification. In strict terms, rape is forcible vaginal/anal penetration without the other person's consent, but in a broad sense it can be any forced intimacy that the person does not want. It violates the sexual self-determination of another. People who are raped are most often subdued by fear and threats rather than physical force. Most victims are women in the 15 to 25 age group, but it can happen at any age.

The **myths** about rape are especially dangerous:

*"Date rape doesn't happen in communities like this."
*This is not true.*

*"It cannot happen to me."
*This is not true. It can.*

*"Women are asking for it by their dress/actions."
*No one asks to be raped.*

116

*"It wasn't rape because she didn't resist."
*It's difficult to fight with someone you thought was a nice person.*

*"Women who say 'no' really don't mean it."
*The word "NO" doesn't change. It means no, negative.*

*"If he pays for the date, she owes him something."
*This does not mean he has a right to force sex.*

The most common form of rape involves a dating or acquaintance situation, although it is often the most difficult to prove. "Date rape" or "acquaintance rape" is most likely to go unreported due to pressure not to involve police and victims' fear of public exposure or causing an embarrassing situation for themselves.

If you or someone you know is raped, here are some things you should do:

1. Contact a friend or group such as a rape crisis center in your area for support. Such help is usually available 24 hours a day, offering free, confidential services to victims.
2. Seek medical attention as soon as possible. All injuries are not immediately apparent (internal injury, STI, pregnancy), so all rape victims are encouraged to obtain a medical exam.
3. Do not bathe, douche, or wash your clothing if there is any possibility that you will report the crime, because you may destroy evidence. Bring a clean change of clothing with you to the hospital. A gynecological exam will be done.
4. You have the option of reporting the crime to the police. Try to remember as many details about the incident and the assailant as possible (actions, clothing, jewelry, scars, facial features, voice, vehicle, time, place). You also have the option of withdrawing from the legal proceedings.
5. If you don't wish to report to the police, you may file a third-party report through your local rape crisis center, which will then call the police and give them information about the assailant. This allows you to remain anonymous, while providing police with information that may help identify a multiple rapist.

## SUGGESTIONS FOR WOMEN

Although there is no way to guarantee you won't be raped, here are a few suggestions to help minimize the chance.

- Be aware that rape can happen to you.
- Learn to be assertive.
- Avoid dangerous or uncomfortable situations—like getting a ride home from a party with someone you hardly know or don't trust, or getting drunk at a party with people you don't know.
- Follow your intuition. If you're uncomfortable in a situation, leave.
- Avoid men with violent tempers, who won't take "no" for an answer, or who don't respect you as a person with your own rights and feelings.

As you can see, there are things that can be done to help prevent rape. But in order to eliminate rape we must look at the cause, not the symptoms. Rape is a crime generally committed by men as a class on women as a class. It is a form of social control. The intimidation that rape imposes on women is phenomenal. Society has unwittingly set up a "rape schedule" for women to live by, with a universal curfew and many unwritten rules about walks alone at night or leaving a bar with someone they just met. Many women understand that if they are raped during "rule violating" times, the man often escapes conviction and the woman must take the blame. "It's her fault. Why was she out at 2:00 A.M. knowing she was risking rape? Rape is her penalty."

It will take more than telling women to stay in at night and putting extra lights in parking lots to help. Such actions only serve to confine and restrict women. Those things may decrease rape, but they won't eliminate it. To work toward eliminating rape, we need to deal with the system that teaches male domination and devalues women. Such programs as Men Against Rape, Men Stopping Rape, and Men Against Violence Against Women are a step in the right direction, offering suggestions for men to eliminate rape.

## SUGGESTIONS FOR MEN

- Recognize that the ultimate solution is up to you. It's men who rape, and men who can stop it.
- Any woman has a right to say "no"—if you persist, you're hurting her and breaking the law.
- Learn to see women as your equal, to respect them.
- Develop friendships with women.
- Talk to your male friends about this issue.
- Join your local Men Stopping Rape group or a similar program.

For more information on rape, contact your local rape crisis center or one of the programs mentioned here.

## SEXUAL ABUSE

The majority of children who are sexually abused are the victims of someone the child knows: fathers, stepparents, or babysitters. Often the child does not report sexual abuse to another adult because the molester may have the child "swear to God" not to tell or may threaten to beat or kill the child if she or he says anything to anyone.

It is important to let children know that their private parts are just that—private. If a child reports a molestation to you, be careful to reassure the child that it is **not** his or her fault. *A child never provokes a sexual encounter with an adult.* Children almost never lie about being abused—hear them out no matter how doubtful you feel. Tell the child that God does not listen to oaths made in this situation and that the child will be protected from the person who molested him or her.

Many people who are molested as children are afraid, even as adults, to tell anyone, because they feel responsible for the act. The person bottles up guilt and anger, possibly causing himself or herself psychological harm. It is better to tell someone—a friend, relative, or counselor—than to hold these feelings inside. A child never asks to be sexually abused. Molestation is an abusive act by an adult who takes advantage of his or her authoritative position over an **innocent child**.

## SEXUAL HARASSMENT

Sexual harassment is coercion of a person to obtain sexual favors. It includes sexist comments, fondling and touching, and sexual favors in return for promotions or better grades. It may occur to both men and women, but in most cases it is the male who tends to be the aggressor because men are usually in positions of greater power than women. Sexual harassment is widespread. Although it is not openly discussed, recent surveys have indicated that many women have experienced some sort of harassment at school or in their workplace.

As with other sexual issues, there are many myths surrounding sexual harassment, such as these: If a woman really wants to discourage it, she can; most charges are false; and women should just ignore it when it occurs. The reality is that many men believe women mean "yes" when they say "no" and therefore may not accept a woman's refusal; women have little to gain from false charges; and in most cases sexual harassment will continue or worsen if ignored.

If you or someone you know is sexually harassed, and confronting the individual has not improved the situation, there are places you may go for help. Contact the Office of Human Resources or Equal Opportunity Office at your college or place of employment.

## FAQS

### 1. When does "no" mean "yes"? Male, Senior

*"No" means no, no way, negative, no thanks, not now; it never means "yes." If you are referring to a situation where a woman says "no" to sex or sexual intimacy, yet seems like she may be willing to go further, ask her. Many women have grown up with the message that it's not okay to say "yes" to sex—if she does express her interest in sex, she's labeled or seen as "easy." If you're not sure what your partner wants, talk about it. You have to have her consent. It is important to know that having sex with someone who says "no" is against the law.*

## 2. What causes a man to rape a woman? Female, First-Year

*Many reasons, including issues of power and control. A person that would commit such an act displays complete disregard for another person and his/her right to control one's own body.*

## 3. What is the percentage of women who have been raped by someone they know? Male, Junior

*About 80% of women who have been raped indicate being assaulted by someone they knew. This is contrary to the stereotype of the strange man who jumps out of the bushes in the middle of the night wielding a knife or gun. In fact, the National Health & Social Life Survey found that 46% of women were in a love relationship with the man who forced them into sex; 22% knew the man well; and 19% said he was an acquaintance.*

## 4. How should I react to meeting the guy that "date-raped" me three years ago? Should I hate him? Try to be civil? What should I do? Female, Senior

*I think you should do what feels right to you—be honest with yourself. Naturally, you have some very negative feelings. I would not encourage you to pretend that everything is just fine between the two of you. In fact, I would make it clear that things are NOT OKAY between you. I'm curious: Does he realize what he did to you and how it has affected you? Some women I have worked with in the past have found it helpful to write the guy a letter—spelling out exactly how the rape affected them. Also, have you ever talked to anyone about this? If not, I would recommend you call your local counseling center to meet with one of their staff or, if you prefer to be more anonymous, you could call your local Rape Response Service. Many women find it helpful to talk to someone who can offer support. It sounds like a very uncomfortable situation to be in. I'm sorry you have to deal with it at all.*

## 5. My friend says she was raped and I honestly do not know what to do to help her or where to turn for

**help—to help me help her. She is not going to classes and is very depressed . . . she stays inside our room now all the time and refuses to go out to parties or anywhere. Female, Junior**

*I would suggest contacting the Dean of Students, as well as the public safety/police office, the campus health center, and your campus counseling center. If you live in a residence hall, contact the hall director or the head of residence life. Each of these offices can assist her, as well as assist you in helping her. She needs to know her options in terms of who can help her legally, medically, and emotionally. Many universities now employ sexual assault advocates or counselors, so I would check to see if you have such a person on your campus, or check out the local phone book for a Rape Crisis Center in your community. Sexual assault is a crime and while she needs legal assistance to understand her rights, she also needs medical and emotional assistance. Good for you for being her friend and wanting to help. Believing her is a great first step. Listening, being there, and being patient with her are all going to help. Let's hope your campus is able to respond—they are obligated to help her, but they need to know about this in order to respond. It is up to her to notify someone within the university system so that her situation can be dealt with appropriately. You will be a big help to her by contacting the various offices initially to find out what she needs to do and what role each office might play in assisting her. Best wishes.*

6. **How can a woman say "no" to a guy and convey to him that she really means it? Female, Sophomore**
*A simple "no" will usually suffice. It is easier to say "no" before you are both sexually aroused. It helps to be clear with yourself first about what you are wanting and what your limits are.*

7. **From the age of 7 to age 12 my uncle played what he called a "game" with me. He would do sexual things to me in the guise of some sort of play. He warned me that if anyone ever knew about the game they would know what a bad girl I was. I knew something wasn't right about the whole thing, but I was too young to**

know what it was. *I've never told anyone what happened.* As I got older I heard and read stories about situations similar to mine. The term used to describe it was "sexual abuse." This confused me because I had always tried to brush the whole thing off as "no big deal." The more I heard about "sexual abuse" and its effects, the closer I came to breaking my silence. However, I have not done so yet, because sometimes I think, "What's the big deal? It's not that bad." Recently something happened that only validated these thoughts. In one of my classes we discussed child abuse. The professor talked about three kinds of abuse: physical, emotional, and neglect. Sexual abuse was not even mentioned!! This just reinforced my thinking that maybe it's not a kind of abuse. I guess all of these "victims" *are* just dwelling on some insignificant event from the past. After all, if it's not even talked about in a lecture on child abuse, it must be no big deal, right? Now I feel I'm not going to tell anyone, I'm just going to go on with my life and try to forget about my uncle. **Female, Sophomore**

*Thank you for sharing your experience. I would like to say that I'm sorry sexual abuse wasn't included or emphasized in your class, since it is certainly viewed as a form of abuse and as a source of pain and confusion for many students. Believe me—you aren't alone! I also think talking can be helpful—that's when the healing often begins. Ignoring our past won't make it go away. If you should change your mind and decide you would like to talk with someone, contact your college or community counseling center; they are there to assist you. In the meantime, I would recommend reading,* The Courage to Heal *by Bass and Davis. Best wishes.*

8. **My girlfriend just told me she was raped when she was in high school by a guy she knew. How can I help her? I don't know what to say. Male, Senior**

*I think one of the biggest things you can do is to just be there for her as a support. Take pride in the fact that she feels comfortable enough with you to share such a difficult experience from her past. Finding ways to convey your feelings for her will be important. Some things to say might include: "I am sorry this happened to you," "Thank you for sharing this with me," and "If you want to talk more about this, I am here." Allowing her to talk about the assault, if she is willing and able to discuss it, may be useful for you in terms of understanding the way it has impacted her relationships with others.*

## 9. Does rape only happen to females? How is it possible for men to be raped? Male, First-Year

*Many of us have grown up thinking that rape happens only to women. It happens to men too. Research suggests 10 to 15% of males will be assaulted at some in their life. Unfortunately, men are less likely to report rape. What we do know is that men share many of the same feelings as female sexual assault survivors, including shock, denial, guilt, powerlessness, anger, and fear of not being believed. If male rape survivors think it only happens to women, they may feel isolated and alone. It is important that we recognize that men and boys can be sexually assaulted, so that they can find the support they need to move forward.*

## 10. What do people mean when they say, "Rape is not sex—it is violence"? Male, Sophomore

*If you ask someone who was raped about the assault, typically they do not see it as anything resembling sex. What many survivors talk about is the fear, loss of control, force, and total disregard and lack of respect by the rapist. It does not resemble what one might think of in terms of an intimate sexual relationship where there is love, respect, pleasure, care, and concern for the other person. Someone once said, "If I hit you over the head with a rolling pin, you wouldn't call it cooking, would you?" I think that applies when talking about sexual assault. Sex is the vehicle, but not the goal.*

## CONCLUSION

I hope this book, an effort to be informative about sexuality, has not only increased your intellectual and physical awareness but also helped you to develop a stronger awareness of yourself and a higher level of self-esteem. Each person is an individual and therefore valuable. There is no one in the world just like you. You are unique.

For more information on any topic covered, the following websites may be of service to you.

**Note: Some websites may no longer be current since the publication of this book.**

# RESOURCES WEBSITES

## PROFESSIONAL ORGANIZATIONS FOCUSING ON SEXUALITY

Advocates for Youth **www.advocatesforyouth.org**

Alan Guttmacher Institute **www.agi-usa.org**

American Association of Sex Educators, Counselors, and Therapists **www.aasect.org**

American Board of Sexology **www.sexologist.org**

Archives of Sexology **www.sexology.cjb.net**

Association of Reproductive Health Professionals **www.arhp.org**

Kinsey Institute for Research in Sex, Gender, and Reproduction **www.indiana.edu/~kinsey/**

National Sexuality Resource Center **http://nsrc.sfsu.edu**

Planned Parenthood Federation of America **www.plannedparenthood.org**

Religious Institute on Sexual Morality, Justice, and Healing **www.religiousinstitute.org**

Sex Information and Education Council of the United States **www.siecus.org**

Society for Sex Therapy and Research **www.sstarnet.org**

Society for the Scientific Study of Sexuality **www.sexscience.org**

World Association for Sexology **www.worldsexology.org**

 ## SEXUAL ORGANS—SEXUAL HEALTH—BODY IMAGE

Breast Self-Exam Demonstration **www.komen.org/bse/**

Circumcision Resource Center **www.circumcision.org**

Feminist Women's Health Center **www.fwhc.org**

Focus on Men's Health **www.medicinenet.com/ mens_health/focus.htm**

Focus on Women's Health **www.medicinenet.com/ womens_health/focus.htm**

Men's Health **www.menshealth.com/**

Men's Health Network **www.menshealthnet.org**

National Women's Health Organization **http://gynpages.com/nwho**

Sexual Health.com **www.sexualhealth.com**

Sexual Health Info Center **www.sexhealth.org**

Sexual Literacy **http://nsrc.sfsu.edu/index.cfm? Page=142**

The Clitoris **www.the-clitoris.com/**

Testicular Self-Examination **www.mskcc.org/mskcc/ html/625.cfm**

Women's Health Issues **www.feminist.com/resources/ links/links_health.html**

 ## SEXUAL DECISION MAKING—VIRGINITY—FIRST EXPERIENCE WITH SEXUAL INTERCOURSE

An ethical model for making sexual decisions **www.tiu.edu/ psychology/Model.htm**

Decisions about sex **www.umr.edu/~counsel/ decisions.htm**

Sex has consequences **www.teenpregnancy.org**

SIECUS: Adolescent Sexuality **http://siecus.org/pubs/ biblio/bibs0001.html**

How do you know when you're ready for sex? **www.plannedparenthood.org/teens/ready4sex.html**

## INITIATING A RELATIONSHIP—LOVING RELATIONSHIPS

Data Guru: The Love Test **http://dataguru.org/love/ lovetest/findings/conceptfa.asp**

Guide to Love & Sex **www.loveandsex.com/**

Love & Sex **www.love.ivillage.com/**

Love Test **www.lovetest.com/**

Loving You **www.lovingyou.com/**

Relationship Web **www.relationshipweb.com/index.html**

Romance 101's 100 Questions Love Test **www.rom101. com/lovetest.jsp**

Sex Ed Links on Love & Intimacy **www.bigeye.com/ sexeducation/passion.html**

Sex Etiquette **www.singlescafe.net/etiquette.html**

## SEXUAL THOUGHTS AND BEHAVIOR—SEXUAL SELF-PLEASURING—ORGASM

Atypical Sexual Behavior **www.soc.ucsb.edu/sexinfo/ ?article=activity&refid=014**

Betty Dodson Online **www.bettydodson.com**

Different Loving **www.gloria–brame.com/**

Fetish.net **www.fetish-net.org.uk/**

Jack in World **www.jackinworld.com/**

Let's Masturbate **www.letsmasturbate.com**

Pat Califia **www.patcalifia.com/**

Sex Addicts Anonymous **www.sexaa.org**

Sexual Addiction Recovery Resources **www.sarr.org**

SOLO Touch **www.solotouch.com**

**DATING DILEMMAS—RELATIONSHIP IN CRISIS**

All About Sex **www.allaboutsex.org/**

Ask Isadora **www.askisadora.com**

College Sex Talk **www.collegesextalk.com**

Dr. Marty Klein's Straight Talk on Sex, Love, and Intimacy **www.SexEd.org/**

Go Ask Alice **www.goaskalice.columbia.edu**

How to Have Good Sex **www.howtohavegoodsex.com**

I Wanna Know **www.iwannaknow.org/**

Sex and Relationships **www.thesite.org/ sexandrelationships/**

Sex Info **www.soc.ucsb.edu/sexinfo/**

San Francisco Sex Information **www.sfsi.org/**

Sex Therapy Online **www.sexology.org**

Society for Human Sexuality **www.sexuality.org**

Your Sex Coach **www.yoursexcoach.com**

 **FIGURING OUT (AND TALKING ABOUT) SEXUAL DESIRES—SEX UNDER THE INFLUENCE: ALCOHOL AND OTHER DRUGS**

Communication Skills **www.newconversations.net/**

Erectile Dysfunction **www.nlm.nih.gov/medlineplus/ erectiledysfunction.html**

Female Sexual Dysfunction: A New Medical Myth **www.fsd-alert.org/**

Online Sexual Disorders Screening for Men **www.med.nyu.edu/Psych/screens/disordermale.html**

Online Sexual Disorders Screening for Women **www.med. nyu.edu/Psych/screens/disorderfemale.html**

Sexaholics Anonymous **www.sa.org/**

Sexual Disorders Information Sites on the Web **www3. sympatico.ca/dgotlib/meanstreets.html**

Sexual Dysfunction **www.athealth.com/consumer/ newsletter/FPN_4_27.html**

## PASS WITH CARE | BIRTH CONTROL—PREGNANCY TESTING—ABORTION

American College of Obstetricians and Gynecologists **www.acog.com**

American Society for Reproductive Medicine **www.asrm.com**

Anne Rose's Ultimate Birth Control Links Page **www.ultimatebirthcontrol.com**

Birth Control.com **www.birthcontrol.com**

Education for Choice **www.efc.org.uk**

Fertility Plus **www.fertilityplus.org**

National Abortion and Reproductive Rights Action League **www.naral.org**

National Abortion Federation **www.prochoice.org**

National Family Planning & Reproductive Health Association **www.nfprha.org**

Not-2-Late.com Emergency Contraception **http://ec.princeton.edu/**

Planned Parenthood's Birth Control **www.plannedparenthood.org/pp2/portal/medicalinfo/ birthcontrol/**

 ## SEXUALLY TRANSMITTED INFECTIONS (STIs)— SMART SEX

AIDS Action **www.aidsaction.org**

AIDS Memorial Quilt **www.aidsquilt.org**

AIDS Resource List **www.specialweb.com/aids/**

American Social Health Association **www.ashastd.org**

AVERT **www.avert.org**

Gay Men's Health Crisis **www.gmhc.org**

International Association of Physicians in AIDS Care
**www.iapac.org**

National Center for HIV, STD and TB Prevention
**www.cdc.gov/hiv/dhap.htm**

National Institute of Allergy and Infectious Diseases
**www.niaid.nih.gov/factsheets/stdinfo.htm**

Office of HIV/AIDS Policy **www.dsophs.dhhs.gov/aids/**

STD Prevention **http://cdc.gov/std/**

Safe Sex and Prevention **www.thebody.com/safesex/
stdbasics.html**

Stop AIDS Project **www.stopaids.org**

World AIDS Day Resource **www.worldaidsday.org**

## TRAFFIC CIRCLE AHEAD GENDER/SEX ROLES—SEXUAL ORIENTATION— GENDER IDENTITY

About Gender **www.gender.org.uk/about/**

Bi.org **http://bi.org/**

Bisexual.org **www.bisexual.org/**

Bisexual Resource center **www.biresource.org**

Campaign to End Homophobia **www.endhomophobia.org**

Children of Lesbians and Gays Everywhere **www.colage.org**

FTM International **www.ftmi.org**

Gay & Lesbian Alliance Against Defamation **www.glaad.org/**

Gay Lesbian and Straight Education Network **www.glsen.org**

Gender Education and Advocacy **www.gender.org**

Harry Benjamin International Gender Dysphoria Association **www.hbigda.org**

Human Rights Campaign **www.hrc.org**

International Foundation for Gender Education **www.ifge.org**

Intersex Society of North America **www.isna.org**

Lambda Legal Defense **www.lambda.org**

Lesbian.org **www.lesbian.org**

National Coalition for Gay, Lesbian, Bisexual, and Transgender Youth **www.outproud.org**

National Gay and Lesbian Task Force **www.ngltf.org**

Outright **www.outright.org**

Parents, Families, and Friends of Lesbian and Gays **http://www.pflag.org**

Planet Out **www.planetout.com**

Queer Resources Directory **www.qrd.org/**

Transgender Guide **www.tgguide.com/**

Transgendered Network International **www.tgni.com**

Transsexual Women's Resources **www.annelawrence.com**

Transsexuality **http://transsexual.org**

Tri-Ess **www.tri-ess.com**

Youth Assistance Organization **http://youth.org**

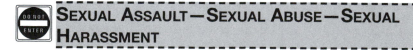

## SEXUAL ASSAULT—SEXUAL ABUSE—SEXUAL HARASSMENT

Abused Men/Boys **www.themenscenter.com/ national/national01.htm**

Acquaintance Rape **www.wcstx.com/friendrp.htm**

Athletes for Sexual Responsibility **www.umaine. edu/athletesforsexualresponsibility**

Incest Survivors Resource Network International (ISRNI)
**www.jericho.org/~jericho/_isrni.html**

Male Athletes Against Violence **www.umaine.edu/maav**

Men Can Stop Rape **www.mencanstoprape.org**

Men Stopping Rape **www.danenet.wicip.org/msr**

Men Stopping Violence **www.menstoppingviolence.org**

National Organization on Male Sexual Victimization
**www.malesurvivor.org**

Rape Abuse and Incest National Network (RAINN)
**www.rainn.org**

Security on Campus **www.securityoncampus.org**

Sexual Harassment **www.ncjrs.org/txtfiles/harass.txt**

Sexual Harassment Resource
**www.sexualharassmentpolicy.com**

Victims of Incest Can Emerge Survivors (VOICES)
**http://www.voices-action.org**

White Ribbon Campaign **www.whiteribbon.ca**

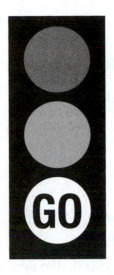

## FOR FURTHER READING

**STOP**  SEXUAL ORGANS—SEXUAL HEALTH—BODY IMAGE

Angier, N. (1999). *Woman: An intimate geography.* Boston: Houghton Mifflin.

Bechtel, S. (1993). *The practical encyclopedia of sex and health.* Emmaus, PA: Rodale Press.

Bechtel, S. (1997). *Sex: A man's guide.* Emmaus, PA: Rodale Press.

Boston Women's Health Collective. (1998). *Our bodies, ourselves for the new century: A book by and for women.* New York: Simon & Schuster.

Diagram Group. (1983). *Man's body.* New York: Bantam Books.

Diagram Group. (1983). *Woman's body.* New York: Bantam Books.

Ensler, E. (1998). *The vagina monologues.* New York: Villard Books.

Gilbaugh, J. (1993). *Men's private parts.* New York: Crown Publishers.

Kilbourne, J. (2000). *Can't buy my love: How advertising changes the way we think and feel.* New York: Simon & Schuster.

Morgentaler, A. (1993). *The male body.* New York: Simon & Schuster.

Northrup, C. (2002). *Women's bodies, women's wisdom.* New York: Bantam Books.

Planned Parenthood. (1998). *Women's health encyclopedia.* New York: Planned Parenthood Federation of America.

Wolf, N. (1991). *The beauty myth: How images of beauty are used against women.* New York: William Morrow.

## SEXUAL DECISION MAKING—VIRGINITY—FIRST EXPERIENCE WITH SEXUAL INTERCOURSE

Bouris, K. (1993). *The first time.* Berkeley, CA: Conari Press.

Hertford, J. (1995). *A pocket guide to loving sex.* New York: Carroll & Graf.

Joannides, P. (2004). *The guide to getting it on.* Waldport, OR: Goofy Foot Press.

Love, P., & Robinson, J. (1994). *Hot monogamy.* New York: Dutton.

Thompson, S. (1996). *Going all the way.* New York: Hill & Wang.

Westheimer, R. (1994). *Dr. Ruth's guide to good sex.* New York: Warner.

Wolf, N. (1997). *Promiscuities: The secret struggle of womanhood.* New York: Columbine Fawcett Books.

 ## INITIATING A RELATIONSHIP—LOVING RELATIONSHIPS

Ackerman, D. (1994). *The natural history of love.* New York: Random House.

Booth, R., & Jung, M. (1996). *Romancing the net: A "tell-all" guide to love online.* Rockin, CA: Prima Publishing.

Carter, S., & Sokol, J. (1990). *What smart women know.* New York: Dell.

Crenshaw, T. (1996). *The alchemy of love and lust.* New York: Putnam.

Crowther, C. E. (1986) *Intimacy: Stategies for successful relationships.* New York: Dell.

DeAngelis, B. (1992). *Are you the one for me? Knowing who's right and avoiding who's wrong.* New York: Dell.

Fromm, E. (1989). *The art of loving.* New York: Harper Collins.

Gordon, S. (1990). *Why love is not enough.* Boston: Adams Media Corp.

Gordon, S. (2001). *How can you tell if you're really in love?* Boston: Adams Media Corp.

Hendrix, H. (2001). *Getting the love you want: A guide for couples.* New York: Perennial Library.

Jankowiak, W. (1997). *Romantic passion: A universal experience.* New York: Columbia University Press.

McSweeney, J., & Leocha, C. (1992). *Getting to know you.* Hampstead, NH: World Leisure Corporation.

Schnarch, D. (1998). *Passionate marriage: Sex, love and intimacy in emotionally committed relationships.* New York: Henry Holt.

Schwartz, P. (2000). *Everything you know about love and sex is wrong.* New York: Putnam.

## SIGNAL AHEAD  SEXUAL THOUGHTS AND BEHAVIOR—SEXUAL SELF-PLEASURING—ORGASM

Barbach, L. (2001). *For each other: Sharing sexual intimacy.* New York: Signet.

Barker, T. (1998). *The woman's book of orgasm.* Secaucus, NJ: Citadel Press.

Boss, S., & Maltz, W. (2001). *Private thoughts.* Novato, CA: New World Library.

Caster, W. *The lesbian sex book.* Boston: Alyson Publications.

Castleman, M. (2004). *Great sex.* New York: Rodale Press.

Dodson, D. (2002). *Orgasms for two: The joy of partnersex.* New York: Harmony Books.

Dodson, B. (1996). *Sex for one: The joy of self-loving.* New York: Three Rivers Press.

Friday, N. (1980). *His secret life: Male sexual fantasies.* New York: Dell.

Friday, N. (1998). *My secret garden: Women's sexual fantasies.* New York: Pocket Books.

Heiman, J., & Lopiccolo, J. (1988). *Becoming orgasmic.* Englewood Cliffs, NJ: Prentice Hall.

McNaught, B. (2005). *Sex camp.* Bloomington, IN: Authorhouse.

Meshorer, M., & Meshorer, J. (1986). *Ultimate pleasure: The secrets of easily orgasmic women.* New York: St. Martin's Press.

## YIELD  DATING DILEMMAS—RELATIONSHIP IN CRISIS

Baumeister, R. F., & Wotman, S. (1992). *Breaking hearts: The two sides of unrequited love.* New York: Guilford Press.

Buss, D. M. (2000). *The dangerous passion: Why jealousy is as necessary as love and sex.* New York: Free Press.

Colgrove, M., Bloomfield, H., & McWilliams, P. (1991). *How to survive the loss of a love.* Los Angeles: Prelude Press.

Cowan, C., & Kinder, M. (1991). *Smart women/foolish choices.* New York: New American Library.

Dowrick, S. (1996). *Intimacy and solitude.* New York: W.W. Norton.

Fillion, K., & Ladowsky, E. (1998). *How to dump a guy.* New York: Workman Publishing.

Firestone, R., & Catlett, J. (1999). *Fear of intimacy.* Washington, DC: American Psychological Association.

Gottman, J. (1994). *Why marriages succeed or fail.* New York: Simon & Schuster.

Gottman, J. (1999). *Seven principles for making marriage work.* New York: Crown.

Learner, H. (1989). *The dance of intimacy.* New York: Perennial Library.

Norwood, R. (1991). *Women who love too much.* New York: Pocket Books.

 ## FIGURING OUT (AND TALKING ABOUT) SEXUAL DESIRES—SEX UNDER THE INFLUENCE: ALCOHOL AND OTHER DRUGS

Altman, C. (1997). *You can be your own sex therapist.* Casper, WY: Casper Publishing.

Comfort, A. (1995). *The new joy of sex.* Westminster, MD: Random House.

Ellision, C. (2000). *Women's sexualities.* Oakland, CA: New Harbinger Publications.

Holstein, L. (2001). *How to have magnificent sex.* New York: Crown.

Kaplan, H.S. (1995). *The sexual desire disorders.* New York: Brunner/Mazel.

Kaschak, E., & Tiefer, L. (2001). *A new view of women's sexual problems.* New York: Haworth Press.

Kleinplatz, P. (2001). *New directions in sex therapy.* New York: Brunner/Routledge.

Milstein, R., & Slowinski, J. (1999). *The sexual male: Problems and solutions.* New York: W.W. Norton.

Ogden, G. (1999). *Women who love sex.* New York: Womanspirit Press.

Reichman, J. (1998). *I'm not in the mood: What every woman should know about improving her libido.* New York: William Morrow.

Renshaw, D. (1995). *Seven weeks to better sex.* New York: Random House.

Silverstein, C., & Picano, F. (1992). *The new joy of gay sex.* New York: HarperCollins.

Wincze, J. P., & Carey, M. P. (2001). *Sexual dysfunction: A guide to assessment and treatment.* New York: Guilford Press.

Winks, C., & Semans, A. (1995). *The good vibrations guide to sex.* Pittsburgh, PA: Cleis Press.

Zilbergeld, B. (1999). *The new male sexuality: A guide to sexual fulfillment.* New York: Bantam Books.

Zoldbrod, A. P., & Dockett, L. (2002). *Sex Talk.* Oakland, CA: New Harbinger Publications.

## PASS WITH CARE  BIRTH CONTROL—PREGNANCY TESTING—ABORTION

Bullough, V., & Bullough, B. (1997). *Contraception: A guide to birth control.* Amherst, NY: Prometheus Books.

Gordon, L. (1990). *Woman's body, woman's right: A social history of birth control in America.* New York: Penguin.

Gorney, C. (1998). *Articles of faith: A frontline history of the abortion wars.* New York: Simon & Schuster.

Hatcher, R. (1998). *Contraceptive technology* (17th ed.). New York: Ardent Media.

Kass-Annesse, B., & Danzer, H. (1986). *The fertility awareness workbook*. Atlanta, GA: Printed Matter.

Knowles, J. (1998). *All about birth control*. New York: Three Rivers Press.

McLaren, A. (1990). *A history of contraception*. Oxford, England: Basil Blackwell.

Riddle, J. M. (1997). *Eve's herbs: A history of contraception and abortion in the west*. Cambridge, MA: Harvard University Press.

Tribe, L. (1992). *Abortion: The clash of absolutes*. New York: W.W. Norton.

Weddington, S. (1992) *A question of choice*. New York: Putnam.

## SEXUALLY TRANSMITTED INFECTIONS (STIs)—SMART SEX

Alyson, S. (1989). *You CAN do something about AIDS*. Boston: The Stop AIDS Project.

Anderson, P. B., deMauro, D., & Noonan, R. J. (1992). *Does anyone remember when sex was fun? Positive sexuality in the age of AIDS*. Dubuque, IA: Kendall/Hunt.

Brandt, A. (1985). *No magic bullet: A social history of venereal disease in the United States since 1880*. New York: Oxford University Press.

Breitman, P., Knutson, K., & Reed, P. (1987). *How to pursuade your lover to use a condom*. Rocklin, CA: Prima Publishing.

Cohen, M. R., & Doner, K. (1998). *The HIV wellness sourcebook*. New York: Owls Books.

Eng, T. R., & Butler, W. T. (1997). *The hidden epidemic: Confronting sexually transmitted infections*. Washington, DC: National Academy Press.

Hansfield, H. H. (1992). *Color atlas and synopsis of sexually transmitted diseases*. New York: McGraw-Hill.

Holmes, K. K., Mardh, P. A., Stamm, W. E., Sparling, F., & Wasserheit, J. (1998). *Sexually transmitted diseases.* New York: McGraw-Hill.

Monif, G. R. (1996). *Understanding genital herpes.* New York: Parthenon Publishing Group.

Morse, S. A. (1996). *Atlas of sexually transmitted diseases and AIDS.* St. Louis, MO: Mosby-Year Book.

Nevid, J. A., & Nevid, J. S. (1997). *Choices: Sex in the age of STDs.* Boston: Allyn & Bacon.

Shilts, R. (1987). *And the band played on: Politics, people, and the AIDS epidemic.* New York: St. Martin's Press.

Ward, D. E., & Krim, M. (1998). *The Amfar AIDS handbook.* New York: W.W. Norton.

Watstein, S. B., & Chandler, K. (1998). *The AIDS dictionary.* New York: Facts on File.

Wisdom, A., & Hawkins, D. A. (1997). *Diagnosis in color: Sexually transmitted diseases.* St. Louis, MO: Mosby-Year Book.

## TRAFFIC CIRCLE AHEAD — GENDER/SEX ROLES—SEXUAL ORIENTATION— GENDER IDENTITY

Boylan, J. F. (2004). *She's not there: A life in two genders.* New York: Broadway Books.

Bullough, V., & Bullough, B. (1993). *Cross-dressing, sex and gender.* Philadelphia: University of Pennsylvania Press.

Colapinto, J. (2000). *As nature made him: The boy who was raised as a girl.* New York: HarperCollins.

Fausto-Sterling, A. (2000). *Sexing the body: Gender politics and the construction of sexuality.* New York: Basic Books.

Galliano, G. (2002). *Gender: Crossing Boundaries.* Belmont, CA: Wadsworth Press.

Geller, T. (1990). *Bisexuality: A reader and sourcebook.* Ojai, CA: Times Change Press.

Levant, R., & Pollack, W. (1995). *A new psychology of men.* New York: Basic Books.

Lips, H. (2001). *Sex and gender.* Mountain View, CA: Mayfield.

Loulan, J. (1987). *Lesbian passion: Loving ourselves and each other.* San Francisco: Spinsters.

MacKenzie, G. (1994). *Transgender nation.* Bowling Green, OH: Popular Press.

McNaught, B. (1997). *Now that I'm out, what do I do?* New York: St. Martin's Press.

Rider, E. (2000). *Our voices: Psychology of women.* Belmont, CA: Wadsworth/Thomson Learning.

Rust, P. (2000). *Bisexuality in the United States.* New York: Columbia University Press.

Signorile, M. (1995). *Outing yourself: How to come out as lesbian or gay to your family, friends, and coworkers.* New York: Simon & Schuster.

Swan, W. K. (1997). *Gay/lesbian/bisexual/transgender public policy issues.* New York: Harrington Park Press.

Tannen, D. (1990). *You just don't understand: Men and women in communication.* New York: Morrow.

## SEXUAL ASSAULT—SEXUAL ABUSE—SEXUAL HARASSMENT

Bart, P., & O'Brien, P. (1985). *Stopping rape: Successful survival strategies.* New York: Pergamon Press.

Bass, E., & Davis, L. (1994). *The courage to heal.* New York: Harper & Row.

Brownmiller, S. (1975). *Against our will: Men, women, and rape.* New York: Simon & Schuster.

Funk, R. (1993). *Stopping rape: A challenge for men.* Philadelphia: New Society Publishers.

Groth, N. (1979). *Men who rape.* New York: Plenum.

Herman, J. (1997). *Trauma and recovery.* New York: Basic Books.

Maltz, W. (2001). *The sexual healing journey.* New York: HarperCollins.

Paludi, M. A. (1996). *Sexual harassment on college campuses.* Albany: State University of New York Press.

Parrot, A., & Bechhofer, L. (1991). *Acquaintance rape: The hidden crime.* New York: Wiley.

Sanday, P. R. (1996). *A woman scorned: Acquaintance rape on trial.* New York: Doubleday.

Sebold, A. (2002). *Lucky: A memoir.* Boston, MA: Back Bay Books.

Warshaw, R. (1994). *I never called it rape* (2nd ed.). New York: Harper & Row.